# Redefining Single Parenting

## Overcoming Obstacles and Raising Resilient Kids

By
The Self-Help Hub

# Introduction

What's the hardest job in the world? Some might argue it's being a surgeon, a firefighter, or even a rocket scientist. But I believe it's being a single parent.

Let me paint you a picture: It's Monday morning, 5:30 a.m. The alarm clock bleats, the piercing sound cutting through the silent darkness. You groan, hit snooze, and roll over, just begging for a few more minutes of sleep. But then you remember—you don't have that luxury. In the room next door, your toddler is stirring. You can hear the faint sounds of her favorite stuffed animal being tossed against the wall. She's awake, which means your day is starting whether you're ready or not.

You shake off sleep, get up, and rush into parenting mode. Your toddler's diapers need to be changed, she needs to be dressed, and breakfast has to be prepared and eaten before you can even think about getting yourself ready. After breakfast, it's a whirlwind of packing lunches, getting dressed, dropping off at daycare, and then it's off to work.

Work is your only respite, but it's also a source of stress. You constantly worry about that unexpected call from school or daycare and whether you can afford the next round of groceries or clothing. At the end of the day, you reverse the morning process—pick up, dinner, bath, bedtime stories, and finally sleep. And then, you do it all over again the next day.

This is the reality of a single parent's life. No breaks, no time-outs, and often no back-up plan. But you know what's even more challenging? Trying to navigate all these daily tasks while dealing with the emotional toll of being a single parent. The loneliness, the guilt, the financial strain, the social stigma—it all adds up. It can feel like you're always walking uphill in a storm, with no shelter in sight.

Yet, despite these challenges, you persist. You keep going, driven by an inexhaustible love for your child and the unshakable determination to give them the best life possible.

As a single parent, you carry the weight of the world on your shoulders. You must play the roles of both parents, simultaneously being the provider, the nurturer, the teacher, and the disciplinarian. Your days often feel like a never-ending circus act, as you juggle work, childcare, house chores, and sometimes even further education. There are days when exhaustion clouds your judgment and saps your energy, making it hard to function. Finding balance amidst these competing responsibilities is a constant struggle and often feels like an impossible feat.

Single-income households face substantial economic challenges. As the sole breadwinner, the responsibility of paying bills, meeting daily expenses, buying school supplies, covering health costs, and saving for the future rests entirely on your shoulders. The stress of making ends meet can often leave you feeling overwhelmed and anxious about your financial stability. This anxiety can seep into other aspects of your life, casting a shadow over your overall wellbeing.

Raising a child takes a village, but as a single parent, it often feels like you are an island. The lack of a support network is one of the most challenging aspects of single parenthood. It's not just about having someone to help with the kids or the chores, but having someone to lean on, to share your concerns and victories, to provide emotional backup. The isolation and loneliness can be stifling, making you feel as if you're carrying a tremendous burden alone.

Whether you're a single parent due to divorce, death, or a decision to have a child on your own, there's often a sense of loss or separation involved. This emotional toll can affect both you and your child. You might be grappling with grief, anger, betrayal, or the simple bewilderment of a life that's veered far off the anticipated course. This emotional upheaval can become an undercurrent in your everyday life, affecting your relationships, your work, and your mental health. Amidst the whirlwind of single parenthood, it's easy to neglect your mental health. The stress, the worry, the constant on-the-go lifestyle — it can all lead to anxiety, depression, and emotional exhaustion. Unfortunately, mental health issues are often brushed under the carpet, not acknowledged, or not treated with the gravity they deserve. This silent struggle is a significant issue that many single parents face, yet it's one of the least talked about.

These are the stark realities of single parenthood. They are challenging, complex, and often overwhelming. But acknowledging these challenges is the first step towards addressing them. By recognizing these issues, you're already demonstrating resilience and readiness to seek solutions. This journey might be tough but remember—you are tougher. You have the strength and the power to overcome these obstacles and raise resilient, happy kids. Let's explore how.

The journey of single parenthood can be a daunting one, marked by a unique set of challenges that test resilience, strength, and the power of perseverance. This book, "Redefining Single Parenting: Overcoming Obstacles and Raising Resilient Kids," is crafted to be a beacon of hope and a toolbox of solutions for every single parent navigating this intricate journey.

By reading this book, you will unearth a plethora of benefits designed to bolster your parenting skills, enhance your emotional resilience, and foster a nurturing environment for your children. Let's delve into these benefits.

The book equips you with practical and effective strategies to balance your manifold responsibilities as a single parent. It offers step-by-step guidance on how to handle multiple roles and juggle work, childcare, and self-care without becoming overwhelmed. The tools and techniques provided will help you manage your time efficiently and create a harmonious balance in your life, leading to more fulfilled, less stressful days.

To alleviate financial strain, the book provides financial advice specifically curated for single parents. It will guide you on how to budget your income, save for your child's future, and handle unexpected financial emergencies. The aim is to arm you with the knowledge to make wise financial decisions and strategies that could offer you and your child financial stability and security.

Feeling isolated and unsupported can be an emotional burden for single parents. This book teaches you how to build and nurture a strong support network. From reaching out to family and friends, connecting with fellow single parents, to seeking professional help, the book presents a variety of ways to alleviate feelings of loneliness and receive the support you need.

Navigating emotional stress associated with loss or separation is a significant part of single parenting. This book provides coping mechanisms and emotional healing strategies to manage these emotional stressors effectively. It offers techniques such as mindfulness, stress management, self-care practices, and advice on seeking professional mental health services when necessary.

In acknowledging the mental health struggles that single parents often face, this book offers strategies for maintaining mental health while dealing with the challenges of single parenthood. From recognizing signs of anxiety and depression to seeking help and incorporating mental wellness practices into your daily routine, the book guides you on how to prioritize your mental health as much as your physical health.

The journey of single parenting is as unique as a fingerprint. No two paths are the same, and no two experiences can ever be entirely identical. Yet, there's an underlying fabric of shared challenges and triumphs, a mutual understanding that binds us single parents together. As I share my story with you, you'll understand why I'm not just an author, but someone who's walked in the shoes of single parenthood and emerged stronger at the end of the journey.

As a single mother and the guiding voice you'll hear throughout this book. I've lived through the rollercoaster ride of single parenthood, facing head-on the realities of juggling multiple roles, the strain of financial responsibilities, the challenge of building a support network, and the emotional toll of loss and separation.

When I was thrust into single parenthood, I felt isolated and overwhelmed. I grappled with balancing work and childcare, managing household chores, and dealing with financial pressure — all the while feeling the emotional sting of loss. It felt like I was navigating an unfathomable labyrinth without a guide, constantly hitting dead-ends and struggling to find my way. It was hard, incredibly hard.

Yet, despite the challenges, I learned, grew, and found ways to thrive. I discovered strategies to manage my time efficiently, learned to handle my finances effectively, built a solid support network, and nurtured my mental health. Most importantly, I raised three children who have grown up to be strong, resilient individuals. And that, in my view, is my greatest achievement.

My journey as a single parent took a devastating turn when my 20-year-old son unexpectedly passed away. The grief was unimaginable, and the pain was all-consuming. But it was also a turning point for me. I realized the power of resilience, the importance of emotional wellbeing, and the therapeutic potential of sharing our stories. I transformed my pain into purpose, sharing my experiences and learnings with others navigating similar circumstances.

Over the years, I've also become a dedicated advocate for organ donation. My son's decision to donate his organs brought life to others, a fact that has brought me immense comfort. Today, I use my platform to raise awareness about the importance of organ donation, adding another layer to my journey as a single parent.

All these experiences have given me a profound understanding of the challenges and triumphs of single parenthood. They have equipped me with a wealth of knowledge, insights, and strategies that I've shared in this book.

As I share my experiences, advice, and learnings with you, I hope to become a companion on your journey of single parenthood. Together, we will navigate the complexities, face the challenges, and celebrate the victories. Remember, you are not alone in this journey, and with this book, I hope to walk alongside you, illuminating your path as you redefine single parenting. Let's embark on this journey together.

You are not alone in your journey of single parenthood. "Redefining Single Parenting: Overcoming Obstacles and Raising Resilient Kids" is here to guide you through the complexities, triumphs, and challenges. Imagine a life where you feel empowered and capable, where every problem has a solution, and you have the tools and resources to navigate any obstacle. That's what this book will provide, a path paved with practical advice, emotional support, and realistic strategies. So, don't wait another day. It's time to turn the page and start your journey towards becoming the best single parent you can be. Take the first step by diving into this book – your guide, your companion, your roadmap to redefining single parenting. Your journey begins here. Act now. Embark on your path to resilience, strength, and successful single parenting.

# Chapter 1: Embracing Solo Parenthood

Becoming a parent is an exciting, bewildering, and, at times, overwhelming journey. When you are a single parent, this journey takes on a whole new dimension. The poet, Maya Angelou, once said, "I did my best, and my best was good enough." As a single parent, it is vital to remember that your 'best' is not only enough but is profoundly transformative, both for you and your child.

In embracing solo parenthood, we are not just accepting a role or responsibility. We are embarking on a path of discovery and growth that will be filled with challenges and rewards. We find within ourselves new capacities for love, strength, patience, and resilience, often surpassing what we believed we were capable of.

The journey of solo parenthood is not one chosen by everyone. It may have been a conscious decision or one born out of unforeseen circumstances. Regardless, it is a path brimming with potential and profound lessons. Being a single parent does not imply being alone. Rather, it signifies a unique bond of love, a bond that is strong enough to weather the challenges and uncertainties of life.

This chapter serves as a guide to understanding and embracing the nuances of single parenthood. It aims to illuminate the various aspects of solo parenting, presenting the unique challenges and rewards inherent in the journey. Furthermore, it seeks to empower you with a positive perspective, helping you to realize the strength and capabilities you already possess.

The adventure of parenting, although often demanding, is also filled with moments of pure joy and deep connection. Embracing solo parenthood is about accepting and cherishing these moments, understanding the challenges, and persistently moving forward. As we navigate through this journey, let us remember that each step is an opportunity for growth, for ourselves and our children.

## Understanding Single Parenthood

Being a single parent is not just about raising a child or children without a partner; it's a unique journey that brings an entirely new set of experiences and challenges to the forefront of one's life. As we venture into the world of single parenthood, we open ourselves to a distinctive form of resilience and adaptability that we may not have thought was within us.

Every day as a single parent is like stepping into a world that is both familiar and new. It's familiar because of the universal aspects of parenting: the deep love for your child, the instinctual desire to protect them, the joy of their laughter, and the pain of their tears. But it's also new because, in the absence of a partner, you're the primary source of emotional, financial, and physical support for your children.

The responsibility can be daunting. Knowing that you alone are responsible for the happiness, health, and overall wellbeing of another human being can indeed feel like a heavy burden. But it's important to remember that single parenthood isn't just about the weight of responsibility; it's about the joy of independence, the strength of self-reliance, and the beauty of an unbreakable bond.

Through the eyes of society, single parenthood can often be seen as a struggle, as a challenge, or even as a disadvantage. It's true that single parents face unique difficulties, but it's crucial to remember that these obstacles don't define us. They're merely part of our journey, they're the steep hills we climb to reach the top, the moments of doubt that make our moments of triumph even sweeter. We are not victims of our circumstances, but survivors, warriors, capable of overcoming whatever life throws at us.

Single parenthood is not a one-size-fits-all experience. It differs for everyone, depending on a multitude of factors like financial situation, support network, and the age of your children. Someone who becomes a single parent due to the death of a partner may face different challenges than someone who chooses single parenthood through adoption or assisted reproduction. But, despite these differences, there is a common thread that connects all single parents: resilience.

Resilience is the strength and speed of our response to adversity. As single parents, it's what allows us to face hardships head-on and come out on the other side stronger than before. Our children watch us as we handle difficulties, and in doing so, they learn to be resilient too. They see that life isn't always easy, but it's how we handle these tough times that truly counts.

Acceptance plays a significant role in single parenthood. It's about accepting your situation, not as something negative, but as a different path to the same goal: raising happy, healthy children. It's about understanding that there's no perfect way to parent, there's no right or wrong when it comes to making choices for your child, and there's no single way to define a family. Family is about love, support, and understanding. Whether that comes from one parent or two, it doesn't change the essence of what a family is.

Understanding single parenthood involves understanding ourselves, our limits, and our potential. It requires a balance between being kind to ourselves and pushing ourselves to be better. It involves acknowledging our mistakes, learning from them, and using them as stepping stones to become better parents.

Yes, single parenthood comes with its share of challenges, but it's also filled with moments of joy, love, and growth that are unique to our journey. It's these moments that make the journey worthwhile. As we move forward, it's crucial to remember that understanding single parenthood isn't a destination; it's an ongoing process. It's about continuously learning, growing, and adapting to our ever-changing lives. It's about understanding that we are not alone, and while our journey is unique, it's also shared by millions of others around the world. We are single parents, and we are stronger than we think.

## The Unique Challenges and Rewards

Being a single parent can often feel like a challenging tightrope walk. You're constantly trying to balance your child's needs, your work responsibilities, and your own self-care, all while trying to stay steady and not tip over. The unique challenges of single parenthood can sometimes make the tightrope feel narrower and the fall seem steeper.

One of the most pressing challenges single parents face is the constant demand on their time. With only 24 hours in a day, finding a balance between work, child care, household chores, and self-care can feel like an impossible task. Then, there's the financial strain. For many single parents, managing household expenses and child care costs on a single income is a constant worry.

Moreover, there's the emotional aspect. Raising a child alone means there's no partner to share the ups and downs with, no one to step in when you're tired or unwell, and no one to share the parenting load. This can sometimes lead to feelings of loneliness, stress, and overwhelming responsibility.

However, while the challenges are real and can often be tough, they don't tell the whole story of single parenthood. Alongside these challenges are incredible rewards that can transform your life in the most profound ways.

Being a single parent can instill a deep sense of resilience in you. When you face and overcome obstacles on your own, you realize your strength, your capability, and your resilience. It makes you aware of your own potential and gives you a sense of confidence that you can face whatever life throws at you.

Next, the bond between a single parent and their child can often be extraordinarily strong. When it's just you and your child, you become their main source of support, love, and understanding. This can lead to a deeper connection and a more intimate understanding of each other's needs and emotions.

Then, there's the reward of independence. As a single parent, you're in charge. You make the decisions, you set the rules, and you shape your family's life. This independence can be liberating and empowering, making you realize your potential as a decision-maker and a leader.

The journey of single parenthood is also filled with moments of unexpected joy. The joy of seeing your child grow and flourish, the joy of overcoming a particularly challenging day, the joy of an unexpectedly quiet moment of peace and tranquility. These moments of joy, no matter how small, are the jewels that make the journey of single parenthood worth it.

Being a single parent is about recognizing and acknowledging these unique challenges and rewards. It's about understanding that the challenges are real, but they're not insurmountable. It's about appreciating the rewards, even when they're not immediately visible. Most importantly, it's about realizing that the challenges don't make the journey less worthwhile, they make the victories more rewarding.

The journey of single parenthood, like any journey, is a mix of steep climbs, downhill slopes, and flat terrains. But, remember, every steep climb is followed by a rewarding view. Every challenge you overcome, every difficulty you navigate, every obstacle you tackle makes you stronger, wiser, and more resilient. It's these climbs, these challenges, that shape you as a parent and as an individual.

And as you navigate this journey, remember this: You're not just a parent; you're a role model. Your child watches you, learns from you, and follows in your footsteps. As you face your challenges with courage and celebrate your rewards with joy, you're teaching your child the most important life lessons: resilience, perseverance, and the courage to face whatever life throws at them.

# Developing a Positive Perspective

In this solo parenting journey, having a positive perspective is like having a compass that helps guide us through the challenges and the joys we encounter. It's the lens through which we see our experiences and our reactions to them. It's the voice in our heads that whispers, "You can do this," during the toughest moments.

But let's be honest; maintaining a positive outlook isn't always easy. Life as a single parent can sometimes feel like an uphill climb, and it's natural to feel frustrated, overwhelmed, or even hopeless at times. Yet, it's in these very moments that developing a positive perspective becomes not just helpful, but essential.

A positive perspective isn't about pretending that everything is perfect when it's not. It's not about ignoring the challenges or suppressing the negative emotions. Instead, it's about acknowledging the difficulties, giving yourself permission to feel what you're feeling, and then choosing to focus on the positive elements that exist alongside the challenges.

When we face financial stress, a positive perspective helps us see the opportunities within the challenges. Maybe it's an opportunity to reassess our spending habits, explore new streams of income, or teach our children the value of money.

When we feel the pressure of juggling multiple responsibilities, a positive perspective helps us value our ability to multitask, appreciate our resilience, and give ourselves credit for everything we manage to accomplish each day.

When we feel lonely or unsupported, a positive perspective reminds us to reach out to our support network, explore new ways to connect with others, and value the strong, intimate bond we share with our children.

It's important to remember that developing a positive perspective is a process, not an overnight change. Some days it will feel natural and easy; other days, it might feel like a struggle. And that's okay. It's about making small, consistent efforts each day, and over time, these efforts will add up and make a significant difference.

One way to develop a positive perspective is through gratitude. Regularly acknowledging the things you're grateful for can shift your focus from what's going wrong to what's going right. It can be as simple as jotting down three things you're grateful for each day. These can be big things, like your child's health or your job, or small things, like a warm cup of coffee in the morning or a peaceful moment at the end of the day.

Another strategy is to challenge negative thinking patterns. When you find yourself dwelling on the negatives, take a moment to stop and reframe your thoughts. For example, instead of thinking, "I can't handle this," try thinking, "This is tough, but I've handled tough situations before and I can do it again."

Finally, remember to take care of yourself. Physical health, mental health, and emotional health are all interconnected. Regular exercise, a healthy diet, adequate sleep, and time for relaxation and fun can all contribute to a positive perspective.

Being a single parent is a journey filled with challenges, but also with joy, growth, and resilience. With a positive perspective in our toolkit, we're better equipped to navigate this journey, face the challenges head-on, embrace the rewards, and raise our children in a nurturing, loving environment. It enables us to lead by example, showing our children that while life may not always be easy, our perspective can influence our experiences and our reactions to them.

As we wrap up this chapter, it's essential to remember that embracing solo parenthood is a process, a journey marked by courage, resilience, and a perspective shift. It's about recognizing your strength and learning to see the positives in every challenge. Remember, you're not just a single parent; you're a superhero in the eyes of your child.

But even superheroes sometimes need a team behind them. Even the strongest among us can benefit from a network of supporters, people who provide emotional encouragement, practical assistance, and companionship. This brings us to our next critical topic – building your support network.

In the upcoming chapter, we'll explore the importance of fostering a strong support network as a single parent. We'll delve into who can be a part of this network, how to reach out and build these relationships, and how to leverage these connections for mutual support and growth. So, gear up as we prepare to embark on this important aspect of your single parenting journey.

# Chapter 2: Building Your Support Network

It's impossible to overlook the inherent truth in the African proverb, "It takes a village to raise a child." Single parenting, while rewarding in its unique way, can also be a daunting task. Balancing work, self-care, and the all-encompassing task of raising children can feel like an uphill battle. However, the journey need not be a solitary one. With a strong and reliable support network, single parents can ease their burdens, share responsibilities, and enrich their parenting experience.

Support networks are a group of individuals who provide emotional, physical, and practical assistance. This network can encompass family members, friends, neighbors, or even professional contacts. For single parents, this network serves as a crucial safety net, offering help during challenging times and providing a much-needed sense of community and belonging. The importance of these networks cannot be overstated; they not only offer immediate assistance but also contribute to long-term stability and resilience.

---

Building your support network is like constructing a sturdy bridge. It connects your family to the larger world, enabling a smoother journey through life's ups and downs. A robust support network offers a source of guidance, wisdom, and reassurance, reminding you that you are not alone in your parenting journey.

Navigating the world of single parenting doesn't mean you have to do it all single-handedly. The importance of building and maintaining a support network is paramount. The following sections will guide you in identifying potential support systems and cultivating these relationships for your benefit and the wellbeing of your children. Remember, as you reach out and form these essential connections, you are not only empowering yourself but also enriching your children's lives with the warmth and care of a loving community.

# The Importance of a Support Network

When the burdens of single parenting feel heavy on your shoulders, it's your support network that can provide the pillars to hold you upright. These are the people who step in to share the responsibilities, lighten your load, and provide you with the moral support and encouragement you need to navigate through the various challenges. The significance of a supportive circle cannot be understated. It forms the bedrock of resilience for single parents, offering resources and empathy to facilitate their journey.

A robust support network is crucial on multiple fronts. One of the primary roles it plays is in providing emotional sustenance. Being a single parent often means dealing with a myriad of emotions – loneliness, guilt, anxiety, and sometimes even a sense of failure. At such times, a kind word, an understanding ear, or simply the knowledge that there are people who care can work wonders in lifting your spirits.

Further, single parenting can be incredibly exhausting with the never-ending list of chores and responsibilities. A support network can help share these duties, offering respite and balance. From babysitting when you have a work commitment to helping with school pick-ups and drop-offs, these gestures, however small, can offer tremendous relief.

Support networks also play an integral role in the social development of your child. When your child interacts with different members of your network, they learn to understand and respect diverse perspectives. They witness various ways of problem-solving and dealing with conflicts. This exposure can enrich their social skills, nurturing them into well-rounded individuals.

Additionally, when it comes to making important decisions related to your child's upbringing, having a group of people who know you and your child well can be invaluable. They can provide a sounding board for your thoughts, give useful advice, or offer different perspectives that you might not have considered.

Building a support network also presents an opportunity for you to give back and support others in their time of need. The process of helping others can be incredibly empowering. It can make you feel valued and appreciated, thereby boosting your self-esteem and self-worth.

Financial hardships are a frequent challenge faced by single parents. Here too, your support network can come to your aid. They might help you find better job opportunities, offer financial advice, or at times, provide monetary help.

Moreover, these networks can offer help in emergencies - when your child is sick, and you can't miss work, or when you need to travel out of town suddenly. You can rely on your network to step in and ensure your child's routine is not disrupted.

In essence, your support network can be likened to a multifaceted gem. Each facet represents a different kind of support – emotional, logistical, financial, and more. Together, they converge to create a system of care and encouragement, giving you the strength and resilience to parent effectively and lovingly. Building such a network is indeed a worthwhile investment of your time and effort. As you will see in the following sections, there are different ways to build and cultivate these connections, and doing so can make your parenting journey more manageable and enjoyable.

## Identifying Potential Support Systems

Looking around and identifying your potential support systems is like setting out on a treasure hunt. The gems you discover might surprise you. These could be relationships you already have or new connections waiting to be made. Finding these invaluable allies is not as daunting as it might seem at first. The key is to think inclusively, encompassing a diverse range of individuals and resources that can support you and your family.

Family and Friends

Your primary support system often consists of family members and close friends. These are people who know you and your children well, making them a natural go-to in times of need. From babysitting to advice on handling tricky situations with your kids, they can offer a wide range of support. However, remember that everyone has their strengths and limitations. Your best friend might be excellent at giving advice but not as good when it comes to practical help. Identifying these individual strengths can help you lean on the right people at the right times.

Neighborhood and Community

Your local community can be an excellent resource. Neighbors, especially those with children of similar ages, can be lifesavers. Apart from the possibility of carpooling and shared playdates, they can also provide an understanding ear or a helpful hand in emergencies. Community centers, libraries, and local events are also great places to meet other families and build connections.

Workplace Colleagues and Networks

Your workplace isn't just for professional growth; it can also be a hub for emotional support. Colleagues, particularly those who are also parents, can offer a sense of camaraderie and understanding. Also, many workplaces have programs for working parents, providing resources and creating opportunities for networking.

Parenting Groups and Clubs

Parenting groups, both online and offline, can be a treasure trove of support. These groups bring together parents facing similar challenges, providing a platform for sharing experiences, solutions, and sometimes, even providing childcare swaps. These groups can often offer a sense of belonging and understanding that is hard to find elsewhere.

Professional Support

Professionals such as therapists, counselors, and coaches can offer valuable guidance on navigating single parenthood. They can provide tools to manage stress, build resilience, and improve your parenting skills. Plus, seeking professional help can also aid in maintaining your mental health, which is critical for your wellbeing and effective parenting.

Public and Non-Profit Resources

There are numerous public resources and non-profit organizations offering assistance to single parents. These range from financial assistance and affordable childcare to educational resources and job placement services. These organizations can also provide opportunities to connect with other single parents, thereby broadening your support network.

As you identify these potential sources of support, keep an open mind and heart. Remember, every individual or resource you add to your network is a step towards building a solid foundation for your family. The key is to acknowledge your needs, reach out proactively, and accept help graciously. This proactive approach is not a sign of weakness, but rather a testament to your strength and your commitment to providing the best possible upbringing for your child.

# Cultivating Relationships for Support

Creating a support network isn't just about identifying who can be a part of it. It's about cultivating relationships with these people and resources, nurturing the bonds, and maintaining them over time. Cultivating these relationships is like tending to a garden – it requires consistent effort, patience, and a generous dose of understanding.

Communicate Openly and Honestly

The bedrock of any relationship is open and honest communication. Let the people in your network know about your challenges and how they can help. It's equally important to communicate your willingness to reciprocate the support. This creates a symbiotic relationship, wherein everyone feels valued and important.

Show Gratitude

Gratitude goes a long way in strengthening relationships. Expressing appreciation for help received not only encourages further support but also cultivates a positive and supportive atmosphere. A heartfelt thank you, a note of appreciation, or a small token of gratitude can make a big difference in maintaining and enhancing your support relationships.

Reciprocate Support

Support is a two-way street. While you're navigating the demands of single parenthood, remember that the people in your network also have their struggles. Be available for them and offer your support whenever possible. This sense of mutual support strengthens bonds and creates a sense of unity and camaraderie.

Participate Actively

Whether it's a neighborhood event, a parenting group meeting, or a workplace gathering, active participation can foster a sense of belonging and open up opportunities for support. Such platforms provide a space to share experiences, gain new insights, and build stronger relationships.

Respect Boundaries

While your support network is there to help you, it's important to respect their boundaries. Understanding their limitations and not overstepping those boundaries can maintain a harmonious relationship. This mutual respect makes it easier for people to offer support without feeling overwhelmed or taken advantage of.

Seek Professional Help

In situations where you need specific guidance or help, don't hesitate to seek professional assistance. Counselors, therapists, or coaches can provide valuable insights and tools to manage your challenges more effectively. They can also help in improving your relationship dynamics with your support network.

Invest in Online Connections

In this digital age, online communities and platforms can be a substantial source of support. Participate in discussions, share your experiences, and lend a virtual hand to other single parents. These digital relationships can provide invaluable advice, a sense of companionship, and even practical help.

Cultivating relationships for support is a dynamic, ongoing process. The effort you invest in maintaining these relationships will pay off in the form of a robust, dependable network that stands by you in your single parenting journey. The strength and resilience you derive from this network can be the driving force behind your success as a single parent. Remember, it's your village, and nurturing this village can lead to a fulfilling, joy-filled journey of single parenthood.

As we wrap up this chapter on building and cultivating your support network, let's take a moment to reflect on how crucial this network is for a single parent. It's your village, your lifeline, and your sanctuary. But remember, while your village is there to support you, the central role of parenting, decision making, and carrying out the day-to-day tasks still falls squarely on your shoulders.

With this in mind, we move on to the next pressing issue every single parent faces: balancing work and parenting. It's like a complex dance where you have to constantly adapt your steps to the ever-changing music of life. Some days, you might feel like a maestro, seamlessly juggling all your roles. Other days, it may feel overwhelming, like you are one note away from missing a beat.

But fear not! There are ways to manage this balancing act and even become adept at it. In the next chapter, we will explore realistic expectations, juggle the roles of a professional and a parent, and delve into effective time management strategies. By the end of it, you'll have a roadmap to help you gracefully navigate through this dance of work and parenting.

# Chapter 3: Balancing Act: Work and Parenting

Being a single parent is like being a circus performer, a juggler of sorts, constantly trying to keep multiple balls in the air. You're trying to balance the demands of work, the responsibilities of parenthood, your personal life, and your self-care. And each of these balls represents a significant part of your life, a part you can't afford to drop. It's challenging, it's demanding, and at times, it feels downright impossible.

Just as Jana Kingsford rightly put it, "Balance is not something you find, it's something you create." This chapter will serve as your blueprint to help you create that balance. It's dedicated to helping you navigate the tightrope of single parenting and work, ensuring neither sphere is neglected, and you can be successful in both.

We'll start by redefining our understanding of expectations—those we set for ourselves and those imposed by others. You'll discover the importance of setting realistic goals that recognize the constraints and opportunities of your situation.

Following that, we'll explore the dual roles of being a professional and a parent. This is no easy feat, but with the right tools and attitude, it can be managed. We'll consider strategies that aid in wearing both hats simultaneously, and doing so with grace.

Finally, we'll equip you with practical time management strategies to help you better juggle your responsibilities. Time, as they say, waits for no one. But by implementing effective time management techniques, you can make every second count.

There is no one-size-fits-all solution to the perfect balance, because each person's situation is unique. But by applying the concepts and strategies laid out in this chapter, you'll gain a better understanding of how to keep your own balls in the air, confidently and effectively. As a single parent, you are already a performer in the greatest show on earth. Let this chapter guide you on how to make your performance a little bit easier, a little bit more controlled, and a lot more successful.

# Setting Realistic Expectations

As a single parent, you might have found yourself tangled in the web of expectations: those you set for yourself and those set upon you by society, family, and friends. When the demands of single parenting and work merge, it can feel like you're walking a tightrope, with the weight of expectations pulling you from both ends. In this section, I want to share with you how setting realistic expectations can ease this burden, giving you a more grounded and achievable perspective on your life.

One of the first steps in setting realistic expectations is accepting that you cannot do everything. We are often told that we should strive for perfection and that anything less is not enough. But perfection is a myth. It doesn't account for the unpredictability of life, especially a life as demanding as single parenting. By aiming for perfection, we're setting ourselves up for failure, and that can lead to feelings of guilt, stress, and inadequacy. Instead, embrace the concept of 'good enough.' I know, it might sound a little defeatist, but it's not. This doesn't mean you're lowering your standards or settling for less. What it means is acknowledging that you're human, with limitations and needs, and that your best is indeed good enough. It's about letting go of the unrealistic notion of 'doing it all' and instead focusing on doing what you can, as well as you can.

When I was juggling my job and parenting, I quickly realized I couldn't be the ideal employee and the perfect mom simultaneously. I needed to prioritize and decide what mattered most in different situations. There were times when my children needed me more, and other times when my work required more attention. Understanding this helped me set realistic expectations for myself.

Additionally, setting boundaries can aid in managing expectations. This could mean establishing work hours when you're fully engaged in your job and setting aside dedicated quality time for your children. It's essential to communicate these boundaries to your employer, your children, and anyone else involved. This can minimize potential misunderstandings and ensure that your time and efforts are directed where they're most needed.

Furthermore, be flexible with your expectations. Single parenting is full of surprises and unpredictable moments. Your plans might need to change suddenly because of a sick child or an urgent work meeting. Rather than stressing over these changes, adapt your expectations to the situation. Flexibility is a valuable asset in the life of a single parent.

In terms of societal and external expectations, remember that you know your circumstances best. While well-meaning friends or family might have opinions about how you should manage your life, their perspective might not fully understand the complexities of your situation. Use their advice as a resource, but don't let it dictate your actions. Be confident in your choices and decisions.

There's a phrase I've found incredibly liberating: "You can do anything, but not everything." This doesn't limit your capabilities but highlights the reality of our human limitations. As a single parent, you're doing an extraordinary job. You're playing the role of two parents while also striving to achieve your professional goals. Give yourself credit for this.

The expectations you set for yourself should be a compass guiding you, not a yoke burdening you. They should be benchmarks for you to aim for, not unrealistic standards that leave you feeling inadequate. By setting realistic expectations, you're not only setting yourself up for success but also modeling healthy ambition for your children.

In the end, life is not about attaining perfection. It's about striving for progress, growth, and happiness. The expectations you set should reflect this. They should be grounded in your reality, achievable, and focused on what matters most to you and your family. Remember, the goal here is to create a balance that works for you. And that starts with setting realistic expectations. Let this be your first step towards achieving the harmony between work and parenting that you deserve.

## Juggling Professional and Parenting Roles

Being a single parent often means you are the primary caregiver and the primary breadwinner in your household, and these dual roles can feel like two full-time jobs. Balancing professional and parenting roles is not a small task. It can be challenging and, at times, overwhelming. But believe me when I say, it's a feat you're entirely capable of. In my experience, there are strategies that you can employ to make this balancing act more manageable.

One of the key lessons I've learned is the power of organization. As a single parent, you must juggle multiple responsibilities and wear numerous hats, making your life a complex puzzle. Having a well-organized schedule is like having a map for that puzzle. It provides you with a clear view of your tasks and responsibilities, helping you manage your time more effectively. A well-structured plan incorporates your work responsibilities, your children's school schedule, extracurricular activities, meal planning, chores, and some self-care time for you.

Using digital tools and apps for managing your schedule and reminders can be extremely beneficial. They can help you keep track of deadlines, appointments, and daily chores. And remember, it's not just about scheduling every minute of your day. It's also about planning for breaks, leisure time, and those beautiful moments of doing absolutely nothing. Recognizing and accepting the value of help is another vital aspect of juggling professional and parenting roles. For some reason, we often think that asking for help is a sign of weakness. But it's not. It's a sign of strength. It takes courage to acknowledge that you can't do everything on your own, and there's nothing wrong with that. Look for support in your network. It can be your family, friends, neighbors, or a professional caregiver.

Additionally, if your employer offers flexible work options, take advantage of them. Options like telecommuting, flexible hours, or job-sharing can provide you with the freedom to adjust your work schedule to fit your parenting responsibilities. Communicate openly with your employer about your situation. Most employers will understand and try to accommodate your needs.

Switching hats between professional and parent roles can be mentally taxing. Try to create some rituals to mark the shift from one role to another. It could be as simple as changing your clothes or taking a few moments of silence. These rituals can help you mentally transition between roles, allowing you to be fully present in each one.

The juggling act of professional and parenting roles can feel like a circus performance, but it's a performance that you're fully capable of mastering. You're stronger than you think, and you're doing a fantastic job. Remember, you're not alone in this. I've walked this path too, and countless others are walking it now. You are a part of a resilient community of single parents, and together, we're unstoppable.

# Strategies for Effective Time Management

Time, my friends, is your most precious asset. As a single parent juggling work and home responsibilities, you might often feel there aren't enough hours in the day. Well, the truth is, the number of hours in a day is not likely to change anytime soon, but how we use those hours is entirely in our hands. With effective time management strategies, you can feel more in control, less stressed, and enjoy a better work-life balance.

First off, let's talk about planning. It is essential to have a clear picture of your weekly and daily schedules. Know your priorities. Not all tasks are created equal. Some are urgent, some are important, and some can wait. An effective strategy I've found useful is the Eisenhower Box, a simple decision-making tool that helps prioritize tasks by dividing them into four categories: urgent and important, important but not urgent, urgent but not important, and not urgent or important. Prioritizing this way ensures you focus on tasks that truly matter.

Next comes organization. Keeping your physical spaces, like your home and workplace, organized can save you a lot of time and mental energy. Know where things are, so you're not spending precious time looking for them. Organize your digital space too. Keeping your emails, files, and digital documents organized can make your work more efficient.

I cannot stress enough the importance of setting routines. Regular routines provide a structure to your day and can significantly simplify your life. They reduce decision fatigue because you already know what comes next. Whether it's morning routines, mealtime routines, or bedtime routines, they create predictability and stability, especially for children.

Let's also talk about the art of delegation. It's not your responsibility to do everything. If there are tasks that can be done by others, let them. Teach your children age-appropriate chores. It's good for them and gives you a bit of a break. If it's within your means, consider hiring help for tasks like cleaning or gardening.

When it comes to work, learn to say no. If you're already juggling a lot, you don't have to take on every new project that comes your way. It's not about being a super-worker, it's about doing your job well and having time and energy for your home life too.

Multitasking might seem like a good idea, but research suggests that it's not. Trying to do too many things at once can lead to mistakes and reduce productivity. Instead, focus on one task at a time. It's about quality, not quantity.

Make use of technology. There are numerous apps and tools designed to help with time management, from digital calendars and to-do lists to apps that block out distractions. Find the ones that work best for you.

Don't forget to plan for downtime. Time management is not about squeezing every drop of productivity out of your day. It's about making your day more efficient so that you have time for relaxation and recreation. You deserve rest and fun.

Finally, be flexible. Life as a single parent can be unpredictable. Sometimes, no matter how well you plan your day, things go awry. When that happens, take a deep breath, adjust your plan, and carry on. Remember, every day is a new day.

Effective time management can make your life as a single parent more manageable. It's not a magic solution, but it can bring some order to the chaos, help you stay on top of things, and free up time for what truly matters - being with your children and taking care of yourself. After all, time is what life is made up of. Let's make the best of it.

As we close the chapter on balancing work and parenting, let's pause for a moment to acknowledge the progress you've made. You're more empowered to take on your responsibilities, better equipped to manage your time, and hopefully, feeling more in control of your life.

But as you juggle work and parenting, there's another crucial aspect of single parenting that demands your attention - finances. It's not the most exciting topic for many of us, but it's an important one. And remember, it's not just about surviving financially; it's about thriving.

In the next chapter, "Financial Planning and Security", we'll explore this crucial topic. We'll discuss how to create a budget that works for you and your family, strategies for saving for the future, and important information about child support and legal rights. Ready? Let's dive into it.

# Chapter 4: Financial Planning and Security

In this journey of single parenting, it's not uncommon to find yourself stretched thin and wrestling with financial uncertainties. This, however, is a battle that we can conquer, and often the winning strategy begins with planning and understanding our financial environment.

There's a profound truth in Epictetus's words, "Wealth consists not in having great possessions, but in having few wants." As single parents, we may often feel the pressure to provide our children with everything - from the newest tech gadgets to lavish birthday parties. But true wealth isn't about the possessions we acquire; it's about understanding our needs, distinguishing them from our wants, and managing our resources accordingly. It's about achieving financial security and independence, regardless of our income bracket.

In this chapter, we'll focus on the essentials of financial planning, and how we, as single parents, can attain and maintain financial security. Financial planning may seem daunting at first glance, particularly when dealing with one income source and multiple responsibilities. However, it's important to remember that it's not an insurmountable challenge but a skill that can be learned and mastered.

We'll start by discussing how to create an effective budget. A budget is a roadmap that guides us in our financial decisions. It helps us understand where our money goes and allows us to make intentional decisions about our spending. It's about more than just paying bills on time; it's about understanding our spending habits, making necessary changes, and planning for unexpected expenses.

Next, we'll explore ways to save for the future. Saving may feel difficult when you're managing a household on a single income, but it's not impossible. We'll discuss practical strategies for setting aside money, no matter how small the amount may seem initially. Remember, every bit adds up and brings us one step closer to financial stability.

Finally, we'll look into understanding child support and legal rights. Knowledge about these topics is crucial because it can make a significant difference in our financial situation. Whether you're on the receiving end of child support or responsible for making payments, understanding the ins and outs of this system is vital.

Throughout this chapter, we'll also hear from other single parents who have found their path to financial stability. Their experiences and advice can provide both guidance and reassurance, reminding us that we are not alone on this journey. Financial security is attainable, and, with some planning and dedication, we can provide a secure future for our children and ourselves. Remember, the goal is not extravagant wealth, but a life where our needs are met, our future is secure, and we are free from financial stress.

## Creating a Budget

A budget might seem like an overly formal term for something that we do in our heads each month: counting our income and then subtracting our expenses. But having a clear, written budget is like having a flashlight in a dark forest - it illuminates the path, showing us where we're going and alerting us to any potential pitfalls along the way.

The first step in creating a budget is getting a clear understanding of our income. If you're employed, your income might be pretty steady from month to month. But if you're self-employed, work part-time, or have irregular hours, your income might fluctuate. In that case, it's best to estimate your income conservatively, using the lowest amount you're likely to bring in. Remember, it's always better to be pleasantly surprised by extra money than to come up short.

Next, it's time to calculate your fixed expenses. These are costs that don't change much from month to month. Think rent or mortgage, utilities, car payment, insurance, and any debt repayments. These are often the "must-pay" bills. Knowing the total of your fixed expenses is crucial, as it tells you the minimum amount you need to earn each month.

After that, consider your variable expenses. These are costs that can change significantly from one month to the next, like groceries, gas, clothing, entertainment, and any other discretionary spending. Here, it's helpful to look back at your spending over the last few months to get an average. Don't forget to include expenses that don't occur every month, like car maintenance or annual school supplies. Divide these costs by 12 to spread them out over the year.

Finally, don't forget to factor in savings, even if it's a small amount at first. Treat your savings as an expense that you pay to your future self. If it's difficult to find room for savings, consider looking at your variable expenses to see if there's anything you can cut back on. Often, we can find little luxuries that, while nice to have, are not truly necessary. This isn't about depriving ourselves, but about making intentional decisions on where our money goes.

Once you have a clear understanding of your income and expenses, it's time to put it all together. Subtract your total expenses (including savings) from your income. If the number is positive, you're living within your means. If it's negative, it's time to reassess your spending and see where you can make adjustments.

Now, creating a budget is only half the battle. The real challenge is sticking to it. One tool that I found useful is budgeting apps. These apps can link to your bank account, track your income and expenses, and alert you if you're getting close to your budget limit.

Keeping your budget visible, maybe even sticking it on your fridge or using a budgeting app, can serve as a constant reminder of your financial goals. When you're faced with the temptation to spend, it can give you the push you need to stay on track.

What's crucial to remember is that your budget is not a prison. It's the opposite - it's a tool that provides freedom. It's the freedom to spend without guilt, knowing that you've accounted for the expense. It's the freedom from worry, knowing that you're living within your means. And most importantly, it's the freedom to build a secure financial future for you and your children.

Creating a budget may seem like a daunting task. But the peace of mind and control over your financial life that it provides are well worth the effort. It's one of the most powerful tools we have in our journey towards financial security as single parents. With it, we can make sure we're meeting our needs, preparing for the future, and still finding room for enjoyment today. Budgeting isn't about restriction, it's about empowerment - and that's a lesson worth learning.

# Saving for the Future

With our budget in place, let's shift our focus to the future. Saving might seem like an impossible task when you're juggling daily expenses, but I want to reassure you that it's not only possible, it's crucial. Every little bit counts and even small amounts saved regularly can add up significantly over time.

The first step in saving for the future is setting clear financial goals. Maybe you want to save for your child's education, build an emergency fund, or even save for retirement. Each of these goals requires a different approach and timeline, but the common element is the need for consistency and discipline.

Let's start with an emergency fund. This is money set aside to cover unexpected expenses or financial emergencies. Life is unpredictable, and as a single parent, you're the financial safety net for your family. An emergency fund acts as a buffer against unexpected costs, such as a car repair or medical bill, that could otherwise throw your budget off track.

Most financial experts suggest an emergency fund should cover three to six months of living expenses. I know this can sound overwhelming, especially if you're just getting started with saving. But remember, it's not a race. Start small, even if it's just a few dollars each month, and gradually increase as your budget allows.

Next, let's talk about saving for your child's education. With the rising costs of education, this can be a daunting prospect. But remember, every little bit helps. You don't have to cover the entire cost yourself. There are scholarships, grants, work-study programs, and student loans to help. But saving even a modest amount can make a significant difference. Consider opening a 529 college savings plan or an education savings account, both of which offer tax advantages for education savings.

Lastly, there's retirement. Yes, it's important to think about our golden years even amid the chaos of single parenting. We spend so much time and energy focused on our children's needs that we sometimes forget our own. The earlier you start saving for retirement, the more time your money has to grow. If your employer offers a retirement plan, especially if they match contributions, be sure to take advantage of it. If not, consider opening an Individual Retirement Account (IRA).

Now, let's talk about how to actually do this saving. One of the most effective strategies is to automate your savings. This means having money automatically transferred from your checking account to your savings account or retirement fund every month. Automating your savings removes the temptation to spend that money and ensures you're consistently contributing towards your financial goals.

Another strategy is to save any windfalls. If you get a tax refund, a bonus at work, or any unexpected money, consider saving a portion of it. This can help boost your savings without impacting your day-to-day budget.

Remember, saving isn't about making huge sacrifices or denying ourselves and our children enjoyment in the present. It's about making conscious decisions with our money and prioritizing our long-term financial wellbeing. As we demonstrate the value of saving to our children, we're also teaching them important life skills that will serve them well in the future.

In my journey as a single parent, learning to save was like learning to drive. At first, it seemed complicated and a little intimidating. But with time and practice, it became second nature. It's a skill that has not only helped me secure a better financial future for my family, but it's also given me peace of mind, knowing that I'm prepared for whatever comes our way. And that, my fellow single parents, is a feeling that's truly priceless.

## Understanding Child Support and Legal Rights

Navigating the legalities of child support can seem like a labyrinth of confusing laws and daunting paperwork. I know I certainly felt that way in my early days of single parenthood. But with time, patience, and determination, I slowly began to understand and navigate this crucial area of single parenting.

Child support is a critical component of a child's financial security. It's the legal responsibility of both parents to provide for their child's needs, regardless of the relationship between the parents. Child support covers necessities like food, clothing, and shelter, as well as education and medical expenses. As a single parent, understanding how child support works can make a significant difference to your financial situation.

Let's start with establishing child support. This generally begins with determining paternity or maternity if it's in question. Then, based on income and custody arrangements, a court will order a certain amount of child support to be paid to the custodial parent by the non-custodial parent. This amount is based on a variety of factors, including both parents' incomes, the child's needs, and the time each parent spends with the child.

Next, let's look at enforcing child support orders. Unfortunately, there are cases where a non-custodial parent may be unwilling or unable to meet their child support obligations. If you find yourself in this situation, know that you are not alone, and there are resources to help you. The Child Support Enforcement Program, a national initiative, assists parents in obtaining child support from the non-custodial parent. They can help locate the non-custodial parent, establish paternity or maternity, establish and enforce child support orders, and even collect and distribute child support payments.

Adjusting child support is also an important concept to understand. Life is full of changes. Incomes rise and fall, jobs are lost and gained, and the needs of children change as they grow. These changes may necessitate a modification of the child support order. If you or the non-custodial parent experience significant changes in your circumstances, you can request the court to review and possibly modify the child support order.

Now let's consider your legal rights as a single parent. These rights can vary depending on your specific circumstances and the laws of your state. However, some common rights include the right to physical and legal custody of your child, the right to make decisions about your child's health and wellbeing, and the right to control your child's inheritance.

Your legal rights also extend to interactions with your child's other parent. For instance, you have the right to limit the non-custodial parent's visitation if it's in the best interest of your child, and you also have the right to move with your child, although this can sometimes be subject to certain restrictions.

If you're struggling to understand your legal rights and responsibilities, I strongly recommend seeking legal advice. Many cities have legal aid offices that offer free or low-cost advice to those who need it. You can also find resources online, including legal guides, forums, and advice columns.

My own experience taught me that understanding and advocating for your child's financial support is a critical aspect of single parenthood. And as difficult as it can sometimes be, it's a challenge well worth taking on. It's about standing up for your child's rights and ensuring they have the resources they need to thrive.

In the end, it's important to remember that while the journey of single parenthood can be daunting, it's also full of opportunities for growth and empowerment. With each challenge we face, from creating a budget to understanding child support, we're not only building a better future for our children, but we're also becoming stronger and more resilient ourselves.

As we move forward, our focus will shift from finances to the heart of what makes us parents - the unique and enduring relationship we have with our children. This bond is the foundation of our family, the source of our greatest challenges, and the wellspring of our deepest joy.

In Chapter 5, we'll explore the many facets of the parent-child relationship. We'll look at ways to communicate effectively, foster a strong emotional connection, and navigate the highs and lows that inevitably come with parenting. It's all part of our journey as single parents, and it's the most rewarding journey we could ever undertake. So, take a deep breath and prepare yourself, as we dive into the nurturing world of the parent-child relationship in the next chapter.

# Chapter 5: Nurturing the Parent-Child Relationship

As Sophocles once wisely remarked, "Children are the anchors that hold a mother to life." In my journey as a single parent, I've come to realize the truth in this ancient wisdom. Our children are indeed the anchors that keep us grounded, they provide purpose and direction, especially during times when life feels like an ocean caught in a storm. This relationship we share with our children is special, it's unlike any other. It's precious, intense, sometimes difficult, but above all, it's rewarding.

However, nurturing this relationship isn't a walk in the park, especially when you're a single parent, dealing with the myriad challenges life throws at you. It requires patience, perseverance, and immense love. The nature of this bond that we share with our kids means that it needs constant attention, openness, and care to flourish.

This chapter is about that bond, about nurturing and strengthening it. We'll explore various ways in which we can foster a healthy parent-child relationship. We'll look at how we can build a fortress of trust, instill a spirit of open communication, and create quality time that strengthens the bond you share with your child.

One of the most critical aspects of single parenthood I've learned over the years is that it's not just about being a good parent but also about being a good listener, a confidante, a friend. In doing so, we lay the foundation of a relationship that's open, honest, and inviting.

Alongside building this trust, we must also strive to create quality time. It's about being present, truly present, and not just physically. It's about creating moments that you and your child will cherish, moments that help you both grow together.

But nurturing a relationship isn't just about creating bonds and making memories. It's equally about encouraging independence, giving our children the space to grow, and allowing them to make their own decisions. This might be difficult, particularly when you're a single parent who's protective of their child. But it's a crucial step in raising resilient children.

Each of these components, though they may seem challenging, work together to create a nurturing environment that encourages your child to grow, learn, and thrive. I invite you to join me on this exploration of nurturing the parent-child relationship. Let's together dive into the intricacies of building trust and open communication, creating quality time, and encouraging independence.

## Building Trust and Open Communication

Trust forms the backbone of any relationship. It serves as the adhesive that holds together the mosaic of human connections. In the context of a parent-child relationship, trust has an even more significant role. It's the cornerstone that supports the growth and development of a child's emotional, social, and intellectual wellbeing.

As single parents, we bear the responsibility of being both the nurturer and the guide, and it's crucial to establish an environment of trust. Building this trust doesn't happen overnight; it's a process, a journey that we undertake together with our children.

In my journey as a single mother, I learned that to build trust, you first need to be reliable. Children find comfort in consistency. Consistent rules, routines, and reactions provide them with a sense of stability, making the world seem less chaotic and more manageable. Try to maintain consistent routines and follow through with the promises you make. If you've promised to attend your child's school play or promised to cook their favorite meal for dinner, make every possible effort to fulfill that promise. These may seem like small aspects, but they are, in fact, building blocks of a trusting relationship.

One of the most effective ways to build trust is through open communication. I realized this early on. After losing my son, my other children had many questions, and so did I. We were all navigating a sea of emotions, trying to find a way to express our grief and confusion. It was during this time that I understood the power of open communication.

Encouraging open communication with your child means creating an environment where they feel safe expressing their feelings and thoughts without fear of judgment or repercussions. Let your child know that it's okay to talk about all feelings – happiness, sadness, anger, or fear.

In promoting open communication, it's crucial that we listen more and talk less. Truly listening to your child demonstrates that you value their thoughts and feelings. It provides them with the assurance that their voice matters, fostering self-esteem and confidence. Remember, communication is not just about talking; it's more about understanding.

Active listening is a skill, and like any skill, it requires practice. When your child speaks, show them that you're interested in what they're saying. Maintain eye contact, ask follow-up questions, and refrain from interrupting. After they've finished speaking, repeat what they've said to ensure you've understood them correctly.

Respect is another vital element in building trust and fostering open communication. To expect respect from your children, you need to respect them first. Value their opinions, give them space to make their own decisions, and avoid undermining their feelings. By doing so, you not only build a strong, trust-based relationship, but you also guide them towards becoming respectful individuals.

Also, it's important to express your feelings and share your own experiences with your child. By sharing your own thoughts and feelings, you're showing them that it's okay to express emotions, and it's okay to be vulnerable. This transparency can significantly contribute to the trust-building process.

Cultivating an environment of trust and open communication might seem daunting, particularly when you're juggling numerous responsibilities as a single parent. However, it's worthwhile. The bond you create through trust and open communication doesn't just contribute to your child's growth; it also gives you a deeper understanding of your child, their thoughts, their feelings, and their unique perspective of the world.

Building trust and fostering open communication is a journey of patience, understanding, and mutual respect. It's a journey that requires time, effort, and an immense amount of love. But it's a journey worth undertaking for the joy, comfort, and strength it brings to your parent-child relationship.

# Creating Quality Time

Time is an invaluable gift we can give to our children. As single parents, it can be challenging to find a balance between our work, household duties, personal needs, and spending quality time with our children. But it's crucial to remember that it's not the quantity of time, but rather the quality of the time we spend with them that matters.

When I say quality time, I'm not talking about extravagant vacations or lavish activities. Quality time can be as simple as sharing a meal, reading a bedtime story, or even going for a walk together. The focus should be on being present in the moment, showing an interest in what they're doing or saying, and genuinely connecting with them.

Early in my journey as a single mother, I found myself feeling guilty about not spending enough time with my children due to my demanding job. It was a painful cycle of exhaustion, guilt, and frustration. But as time went by, I realized that it wasn't about counting the hours, but about making those hours count.

Making the most of your time with your children starts with being fully present. In today's digital age, distractions are everywhere. We often find ourselves splitting our attention between our kids and our smartphones, work emails, or social media feeds. And while it's essential to stay connected with the world, it's equally important to disconnect and give our children our undivided attention.

So, switch off your phone, step away from your laptop, and tune into your child. Listen to their stories, ask them about their day, and show genuine interest in what they're saying. When your child feels heard and valued, it can strengthen your bond and boost their self-esteem.

Another vital aspect of quality time is engaging in activities that both you and your child enjoy. In my case, my children and I shared a love for books. Reading together became our special time, a haven from the hustle and bustle of daily life. It didn't just provide a platform for us to share stories and explore new worlds, but it also opened doors to stimulating discussions about the characters, their actions, and their decisions. Find an activity that interests you and your child. It could be cooking, gardening, playing a sport, or even doing puzzles. The goal is not just to do an activity together, but to create an opportunity for interaction, communication, and connection.

While creating quality time is essential, it's equally important to be spontaneous. Not all quality time needs to be scheduled or planned. Sometimes, the most memorable moments come from impromptu decisions like a sudden picnic in the park or a surprise baking session. And lastly, during this quality time, express your love and appreciation for your child. Words of affirmation can have a profound impact on their self-esteem and their sense of security. Simple statements like "I love spending time with you," or "I'm proud of you," can mean the world to them.

Being a single parent, our time is always at a premium. We're constantly juggling multiple responsibilities. But amid all these tasks, it's crucial to carve out moments of connection with our children. These moments of quality time, no matter how brief, are the threads that weave the rich fabric of a loving, nurturing parent-child relationship. They're the heartbeats of love, assurance, and connection that remind our children they're valued, loved, and cherished.

# Encouraging Independence

Raising independent children is one of the greatest gifts we can give them as parents. Encouraging independence not only helps children develop self-confidence and self-reliance, but it also equips them with the skills they need to navigate life's challenges. As a single parent, fostering independence in your child might seem like a daunting task, but it's a journey that is both rewarding and profoundly impactful for you and your child.

I remember a time when my oldest child was learning how to tie her shoelaces. At first, she would fumble with the laces, her small fingers struggling to make the loops and knots. As a mother, my instinct was to jump in and do it for her. But I held back. I watched as she tried again and again, her face a picture of fierce concentration. After many attempts, she finally succeeded, and the look of pure joy and accomplishment on her face was priceless. That was a pivotal moment for me. It was a reminder that, sometimes, the best thing we can do for our children is to step back and allow them to do things for themselves.

Fostering independence starts with giving children age-appropriate responsibilities. It could be as simple as letting your toddler put away their toys, having your elementary school-aged child pack their lunch, or encouraging your teenager to manage their schedule. By entrusting them with tasks, we're not just teaching them important life skills; we're also showing them that we trust their capabilities.

When we give our children responsibilities, it's natural to expect them to carry out these tasks perfectly. But it's important to remember that they're still learning. There will be mistakes and mishaps along the way. A glass of milk might get spilled, a deadline might be missed, or a chore might not be done up to your standard. When these things happen, treat them as learning opportunities rather than failures. Show your child how to clean up that spilled milk, talk about time management strategies, and guide them on how to do a task more effectively next time.

Encouraging independence doesn't mean leaving our children to figure things out on their own. It means supporting them and providing them with the tools they need to be successful. Be there to guide and support them but resist the urge to take over. Instead, ask them questions to stimulate their problem-solving skills. "What do you think you could do differently next time?" "How could you handle this situation?" Such questions can help them think critically and develop their problem-solving abilities.

As your child grows and becomes more independent, it's also crucial to respect their growing autonomy. Allow them to make choices and decisions appropriate for their age. Do they prefer to wear the blue shirt or the red one? Would they like to play soccer or take ballet lessons? By involving them in decision-making, we're helping them understand the concept of choices and consequences. It also boosts their confidence, as they see that their opinions matter.

Lastly, celebrate your child's achievements, no matter how small they may seem. Each step they take towards independence is a milestone worth celebrating. Encouraging words and positive reinforcement can go a long way in building their self-esteem and motivation.

Encouraging independence in our children can be a challenging journey. It requires patience, trust, and the ability to let go. But as we guide them on this path, we give them the skills, confidence, and resilience they need to grow into capable and confident individuals. And seeing them bloom into their full potential is one of the most rewarding experiences as a parent.

Moving forward in our journey, we must address a significant aspect of parenting that often elicits mixed feelings - discipline. But remember, discipline is not merely about rules and punishment. Instead, it's about teaching our children the difference between right and wrong, helping them develop self-control, and guiding them towards becoming responsible and respectful individuals.

Chapter 6 focuses on "Disciplining with Love and Consistency." We all know that as parents, our role is not just to be our children's friends, although fostering a friendly and open rapport with them is certainly important. But, at the same time, it's our responsibility to set boundaries and ensure that respect is upheld. Let's delve into this intricate part of parenting, exploring how to strike the right balance between offering guidance and nurturing independence, and between enforcing discipline and fostering a loving, trusting relationship with our children.

# Chapter 6: Disciplining with Love and Consistency - Not Making the Children Friends, but Fostering Respect

As a single parent, one of the most challenging and yet essential parts of your journey is establishing discipline. This task becomes especially complex as you strive to provide both parental figures' roles, balancing love, guidance, authority, and yes, discipline. Harold Hulbert's quote beautifully encapsulates this balance: "Children need love, especially when they do not deserve it."

It's crucial to remember that discipline isn't about punishment or control—it's about teaching and guiding your children to develop self-control, responsibility, and respect for others. Too often, the concept of discipline is associated with negative consequences, harsh words, or even punishment. But discipline, in its truest form, is about teaching, not punishment. It's about showing our children the way, not pushing them towards it.

Now, you might wonder, "But isn't it easier and more comfortable to be friends with my children?" Indeed, there's a compelling allure to the idea of being a 'friend' to your child. After all, friends have fun together, share secrets, and enjoy each other's company.

Yet, here's where the path gets tricky. As parents, we're more than just friends to our children. We're their guides, their protectors, and their teachers. While the friend role seems appealing, it can blur the necessary boundaries between you and your child. It's important to be approachable and loving, but it's equally important for your child to respect you as a parent.

In this chapter, we will discuss the importance of disciplining with love and consistency. We will explore practical ways to establish and enforce house rules, handle behavioral issues, and foster an environment of respect. The goal isn't to create rigid, inflexible structures, but to build a home filled with mutual respect and understanding.

# The Role of Discipline in Parenting

As a single parent, you play a myriad of roles in your child's life - caregiver, protector, teacher, role model, and disciplinarian. The act of discipline, while sometimes challenging, is a fundamental aspect of parenting. It helps shape character, develops resilience, and lays the groundwork for a sense of responsibility and respect in your children.

Discipline often gets a bad reputation, mainly when associated with punishment or negative reinforcement. But in reality, discipline is more about teaching your child the difference between acceptable and unacceptable behavior. It's about imparting essential life skills like self-control, empathy, and respect for others. As Harold Hulbert rightly said, "Children need love, especially when they do not deserve it." At the core of discipline, love and understanding need to exist.

One crucial point to understand is the difference between discipline and punishment. Punishment is about imposing a penalty for an offense, while discipline is about teaching correct behavior. It's possible - and indeed more beneficial - to discipline without punishment. Think of discipline as a way to guide your child on the right path rather than as a means to correct their wrongdoings.

The ultimate goal of discipline is to help your child grow into a responsible, compassionate, and well-rounded individual. This goal doesn't mean enforcing a stringent set of rules, but guiding your child to understand why certain behaviors are desired and others are not. It's not about setting a path for your child to blindly follow; it's about helping them understand why that path exists.

Discipline also helps create a sense of consistency and security in your child's life. Children thrive on predictability. They feel secure when they know what's expected of them and what the consequences will be if they don't follow the rules. This security helps them navigate the world around them with confidence.

But how can you ensure discipline in your home is effective and loving, rather than punitive or harsh? That's where the principles of love and consistency come in.

When discipline is rooted in love, it becomes an act of caring, not correction. Love-based discipline isn't about asserting power over your child; it's about helping your child learn from their mistakes and guiding them towards better behavior. It's about showing empathy, understanding their emotions, and teaching them to do the same.

Consistency, on the other hand, is about following through with the rules and consequences you've established. It's one of the most challenging aspects of discipline, especially for single parents juggling multiple responsibilities. But without consistency, children may become confused about what's expected of them, which can lead to more behavioral issues.

It's essential to remember that while maintaining discipline is critical, it should never overshadow the love, joy, and warmth that should be the foundation of your relationship with your child. Discipline should never mean an absence of affection, fun, or heartfelt conversations. It should be a guiding force, not a controlling one.

In essence, discipline is a life skill, a tool that your child will carry into adulthood. It's a guide to understanding the world, engaging with others, and navigating through challenges. It's about instilling values, shaping character, and fostering resilience.

Balancing the roles of being a friend, guide, and disciplinarian can be tricky, but remember, you are not alone in this journey. Many single parents are navigating this delicate balance too. It's a learning process, and sometimes, you might make mistakes, and that's okay. The key is to learn, adapt, and try again. After all, your love for your child is the driving force behind your efforts to discipline. And with that love as your foundation, you're more equipped than you might think.

## Creating and Implementing House Rules

The creation and implementation of house rules can be a cornerstone of effective discipline. It sets clear expectations for behavior and establishes a sense of order and predictability. House rules can also foster a sense of responsibility in your children and provide a framework for resolving conflicts.

But where should you begin? Here are some strategies to help you create and implement house rules that are effective, fair, and easy to follow.

Firstly, involve your children in the process. This might sound counterintuitive but involving your children in the rule-making process can make them feel valued and more likely to follow the rules. Sit down together and discuss what rules are necessary for your home. This discussion will help them understand the purpose of the rules and the benefits of following them.

Keep the rules simple and clear. The aim is not to create an extensive list of dos and don'ts but to establish clear boundaries for behavior. Try to limit your rules to what's most important. A good rule of thumb is to have one rule for each year of your child's age - for instance, a five-year-old should have about five basic rules.

Ensure the rules are specific and understandable. Vague or complex rules can lead to misunderstandings. Instead of "be good," opt for specific actions like "no hitting" or "tidy up after playing." This specificity helps your child understand exactly what is expected of them.

Once you've established the rules, it's time to implement them, and here's where consistency comes into play. Consistency in enforcing rules is critical. If you're inconsistent, your child might become confused or might try to test the boundaries. If a rule is important enough to make, it's important enough to enforce every time.

It's also crucial to make the consequences of breaking the rules clear. Let your child know what will happen if they break a rule. Remember, the aim is not to punish but to teach. The consequences should be reasonable and related to the rule. For example, if the rule is to tidy up after play, a suitable consequence might be that your child can't play with their toys until they've cleaned up their previous mess.

House rules should also evolve as your children grow and their needs change. What works for a preschooler won't necessarily work for a teenager. As your children grow older, you can involve them in adjusting the rules to suit their changing needs and responsibilities.

While it's important to establish and enforce rules, it's equally important to recognize and reward good behavior. Positive reinforcement can be a powerful tool in promoting desired behavior. This recognition doesn't have to be a big reward - a simple acknowledgment or a word of praise can work wonders.

Creating and implementing house rules is not about controlling your child's behavior. It's about setting a framework for respectful and responsible behavior. It's about teaching your child the difference between right and wrong and helping them understand the impact of their actions.

Remember, the goal isn't perfection. There will be days when rules are broken and tempers flare. But don't be disheartened. Consider these moments as learning opportunities - for both you and your child. Each day is a new chance to teach, learn, and grow together.

Throughout this process, remind your child that the rules are not there to make their life hard, but to ensure everyone in the house is treated with respect and kindness. Make it clear that everyone, including you, follows these rules.

Implementing house rules might not be an easy task, but it's an important part of creating a harmonious and respectful home environment. And remember, in this journey of discipline and growth, there's no better motivation than the love you have for your child. Your commitment to their growth and wellbeing will be the driving force behind these efforts. In the next part, we will discuss the ways to deal with behavioral issues, another crucial aspect of disciplining with love and consistency.

## Dealing with Behavioral Issues

Navigating your child's behavioral issues can feel like a complex maze without a clear exit in sight. One minute they're all smiles, and the next, they're having a meltdown in the middle of the supermarket. The complexities can sometimes feel overwhelming, but remember, it's all part of their growth and learning journey.

The most important thing to understand is that behavior is a form of communication. When children act out, it's often because they're struggling to express their feelings or needs. So, the first step in addressing behavioral issues is understanding what your child is trying to communicate.

Take a moment to observe your child. Are there any patterns to their behavior? Do they act out when they're tired, hungry, or not getting enough attention? Understanding these triggers can help you proactively manage their behavior.

It's essential, too, to communicate with your child. When they're calm, talk to them about their feelings and behavior. Encourage them to express themselves and assure them that it's okay to have strong feelings, but it's not okay to act out in inappropriate ways.

When dealing with behavioral issues, consistency is key. Just like with house rules, ensure that the consequences of unacceptable behavior are clear and consistent. Remember, the goal is not to punish but to teach them how to behave appropriately.

Here's where patience comes in. Change takes time, and there will be setbacks. But remember, each setback is an opportunity for learning and growth. Take a deep breath, give your child a hug, and remind yourself that you're both learning.

Don't forget to model the behavior you want to see. Children learn a lot from observing the adults in their lives. If you want them to learn respect, show them what respect looks like. If you want them to learn patience, demonstrate patience.

But what about those times when it all seems too much, when the meltdowns seem endless, or when you've had to deal with the same behavioral issue over and over again? These are the times when it's crucial to have a support network in place. Reach out to family, friends, or a professional. Remember, it's okay to ask for help.

Lastly, always make sure to acknowledge good behavior. When your child behaves appropriately, praise them. Positive reinforcement can encourage good behavior and help your child understand that they've done something right.

Dealing with behavioral issues is undoubtedly challenging, but remember, it's all part of the journey of parenting. The sleepless nights, the tantrums, the endless questions – they're all moments that offer an opportunity to teach and to learn.

And remember, even amidst the chaos of a tantrum or the frustration of a repeated behavioral issue, there is always an opportunity for a hug, a kind word, or a moment of understanding. These are the moments that remind us that love is at the heart of parenting. It's the force that keeps us going, that fuels our patience and our persistence.

As a single parent, dealing with behavioral issues can be particularly challenging. But you're not alone. There are resources available, support networks to tap into, and strategies you can use to navigate these challenges.

And remember, behind every behavioral issue is a child trying to figure out this vast world. So, hang in there. Show patience, show understanding, but most importantly, show love. For it is through love that we find the strength to guide our children through their most challenging behaviors and into their greatest achievements.

Dealing with behavioral issues is a fundamental part of parenting. And as we've explored, the key lies in understanding, communication, patience, consistency, and love. However, parenting also involves addressing more complex emotional issues that arise due to family dynamics, especially in the case of single-parent households.

Now, let's venture into an area that can sometimes be uncomfortable but is extremely important to address - dealing with the absent parent. The impact of an absent parent on a child's life and development can be significant, and as a single parent, it's crucial that we understand how to navigate this sensitive topic.

In the next chapter, Chapter 7, we will explore different scenarios of dealing with an absent parent and provide guidance on how to handle this delicate matter with sensitivity, honesty, and your child's best interests at heart. We'll touch upon how to answer tough questions, how to deal with feelings of loss, and how to help your child cope with the absence of one parent. Let's continue this journey of growth, resilience, and boundless love for our children together. Onward we go!

# Chapter 7: Dealing with the Absent Parent

The journey of single parenthood can be a winding road with unexpected bends and humps, but one of the most challenging aspects can be managing the presence—or absence—of the other parent in your child's life. This chapter is about acknowledging that reality and learning ways to handle it with grace, resilience, and above all, with your child's wellbeing at heart.

Perhaps the absent parent is involved sporadically, or maybe they're completely out of the picture. Either way, their absence is a substantial part of your child's world. It's a topic that can stir up a multitude of emotions, from confusion to anger to sadness, both for you and your child. Questions may arise: "Why isn't Dad around?" "Why did Mom leave?" "Will they come back?" These are challenging inquiries that, as a single parent, you might find yourself needing to address sooner than you'd prefer.

At the heart of this chapter is the idea that dealing with an absent parent isn't just about responding to your child's questions. It involves the larger process of establishing healthy boundaries, both for yourself and your child. It means setting the terms for the absent parent's possible involvement and dealing with the impact of their absence. This process can be tricky, especially when emotions run high, but it's a necessary part of your journey.

In "Dealing with the Absent Parent," you'll find not just strategies, but a sense of understanding and empathy. I've been there, and I want to share the insights and tools that have helped me navigate these challenging waters. This chapter won't erase the difficulties, but it will equip you with the knowledge and confidence to face them head-on. Together, we can ensure your journey as a single parent, and your child's journey into resilience and wellbeing, remain steadfastly on track.

# Handling Questions and Emotions

As a single parent, it's natural to have mixed feelings about the absent parent. It's also normal for your child to feel a wide range of emotions and have a lot of questions about the situation. The first step to navigating this complex terrain is to validate these feelings - both yours and your child's - and understand that they are an entirely reasonable response to the circumstances.

There's no rulebook that can precisely dictate the timing or nature of the questions your child might have. They can spring up unexpectedly during an otherwise ordinary day, or be the recurring theme of many heartfelt conversations. Some questions will be simple and factual, while others may echo profound emotions your child is grappling with. Questions like, "Why doesn't Daddy live with us?" or "Does Mommy not love us anymore?" are loaded with longing, confusion, and sometimes, hurt.

The challenge here is to respond with honesty and empathy, while keeping the answers age-appropriate and respectful towards the absent parent. This is not about hiding the truth or sugarcoating reality, but rather about presenting it in a way that your child can comprehend and process without feeling overwhelmed or distressed. For instance, you might say, "Daddy lives somewhere else because we disagreed on a lot of things, but he still loves you very much."

However, it's not just about answering your child's questions. It's also about handling the emotions that come along with these conversations. Acknowledge your child's feelings. If they're angry, tell them it's okay to feel that way. If they're sad, let them know you understand. Give them the space to express their feelings and assure them that their emotions are valid.

In the midst of these discussions, you might find your own emotions coming to the surface. It's normal to feel sadness, frustration, or even guilt over the absent parent. Take time to address these feelings. Lean on your support network, write in a journal, or talk to a therapist. It's crucial that you process your own emotions so that you can effectively help your child navigate theirs.

Remember, children often mirror the adults in their lives. If they see you handling your emotions healthily, they will learn to do the same. This is not about being invulnerable, but about modeling resilience, understanding, and emotional health.

In the end, dealing with questions and emotions is an ongoing process. There will be moments of clarity and moments of confusion, times when it feels like you've got it all figured out and times when you're at a loss for what to say or how to feel. That's all part of the journey. The goal is not to strive for perfection but to foster open communication, mutual respect, and emotional authenticity with your child.

I want you to know that it's okay to feel uncertain or overwhelmed at times. It's okay to not have all the answers. It's okay to feel and to let your child see your feelings. You are human, after all. In these moments, remember that it's not about being perfect, but about being present - present in your child's life, present in your emotions, and present in your journey of single parenting.

# Setting Healthy Boundaries

The significance of setting boundaries is often underrated, but it plays a key role in maintaining a balanced relationship with the absent parent and for the overall wellbeing of your child. Boundaries help to clarify what is acceptable behavior and what is not, and they provide a sense of security and predictability in relationships. They also protect your emotional space and can help prevent miscommunication and misunderstandings.

Boundaries may involve practical aspects such as visitation schedules, communication methods, and financial responsibilities, or emotional aspects such as respectful conversation and safeguarding the child's feelings. It's crucial to set these boundaries early and consistently, to provide a stable and predictable environment for your child.

A healthy boundary can look like setting specific days and times for the absent parent to visit or call, ensuring that your child has a routine and knows what to expect. It could also mean deciding on the way the absent parent communicates with you, such as via email or text messages, to avoid unnecessary conflict or confusion.

Financial responsibilities should be clearly outlined too. This includes child support payments, sharing of school or extracurricular costs, and how unexpected expenses will be handled. This clarity can help avoid potential disputes and ensure the financial stability of your child.

Boundaries are also important in conversations about the absent parent. Establish clear guidelines about how the absent parent is spoken about in front of the child. Negative comments or discussions about legal matters should be avoided. This not only shows respect towards the absent parent but also protects your child from undue stress or confusion.

While setting these boundaries, it's important to keep in mind that they are not meant to create a barrier between your child and the absent parent, but rather to foster a healthy and stable environment for your child. Always keep your child's best interests at heart when establishing these guidelines.

As much as setting boundaries is important, enforcing them is equally crucial. You must be prepared to assert these boundaries if they are crossed. This could involve having tough conversations or making difficult decisions, but remember, your primary responsibility is the wellbeing of your child.

I know that setting boundaries might seem challenging, especially when dealing with an uncooperative or disagreeable ex-partner. It's okay to seek help. Legal advice can be beneficial in setting more formal boundaries, such as custody arrangements or financial responsibilities. Counselors or therapists can also provide guidance on handling difficult conversations and managing emotions during this process.

Creating these boundaries is an act of care - for your child and for yourself. It's about designing a framework within which your child can have a healthy relationship with both parents. It's also about safeguarding your own emotional health, ensuring that the complexities of your relationship with the absent parent don't overflow into your daily life.

Setting boundaries won't always be easy. There will be moments of resistance, discomfort, and doubt. But remember, this isn't just about the here and now. It's about laying a strong foundation for the future - a future where your child feels secure, understood, and loved. It's about showing your child that relationships, even complicated ones, can be navigated with respect, communication, and clear expectations.

In essence, setting healthy boundaries isn't just a task to be ticked off your to-do list; it's a continuous journey of respect, communication, and care. It's a journey that requires courage, patience, and resilience - qualities that you, as a single parent, have in abundance.

## Ensuring Emotional Stability

Emotional stability is a cornerstone of every child's healthy development. As single parents, we are often their primary source of emotional support. While the journey can feel overwhelming, please remember that your commitment to your child's emotional well-being is a profound act of love. Here are a few strategies I've found helpful in fostering emotional stability.

First, let's talk about open communication. Your child might have a flurry of emotions about the absent parent. They may feel sadness, anger, confusion, or even guilt. Encourage them to express these feelings. Ask them about their day, their thoughts, their feelings, and let them know they can come to you with any concerns. Keep your emotions in check during these discussions. It's essential to respond with patience and understanding, even when it's tough.

Next, you should normalize the expression of emotions. Sometimes, children may feel they need to hide their feelings or be "strong." Show them that it's perfectly okay to feel their emotions and express them in healthy ways. Whether it's crying, talking, or engaging in an activity that helps them relax, it's vital that they understand that feelings are a natural part of the human experience.

Consistency is another key aspect of emotional stability. Children thrive on routines as they provide a sense of security and predictability. Try to maintain a consistent schedule for meals, homework, leisure activities, and bedtime. However, remember that the aim isn't to regiment every minute, but to create a flexible structure that provides a comforting rhythm to their days.

During this time, it's also important to foster their self-esteem. Children might internalize the absence of a parent as a reflection on their self-worth. Reassure them that they are loved and valued. Celebrate their achievements, and more importantly, their efforts. Teach them that their worth is not dependent on anyone else's presence or absence.

A crucial part of ensuring emotional stability is taking care of your emotional health. As the saying goes, you can't pour from an empty cup. Practice self-care, find healthy outlets for your stress, and seek support when you need it. Remember, it's not selfish to take care of yourself; it's necessary. Your emotional well-being has a direct impact on your child's emotional state.

Finally, consider seeking professional help if needed. If your child is struggling significantly with the absence of the other parent, a trained therapist or counselor can provide invaluable support. Therapy can offer them a safe space to express their emotions and equip them with coping skills to navigate this challenging situation.

Each day, each challenge, each triumph is a step forward. And with each step, you're not just ensuring your child's emotional stability; you're teaching them resilience, empathy, and emotional intelligence. You're showing them that even in the face of challenges, they have the strength to thrive. And that, my friend, is one of the greatest gifts you can give your child.

# Chapter 8: Health and Self-Care for Single Parents

"An empty lantern provides no light. Self-care is the fuel that allows your light to shine brightly." - Unknown

In the hectic whirlwind of single parenting, it's easy to forget the person at the eye of the storm - you. As a single parent, you are the heart and backbone of your family. Your wellbeing, both physical and mental, is essential not just for you, but for your children too. Hence, nurturing your health and practicing self-care are far from being acts of selfishness; they are the most profound expressions of love you can show to your children.

This chapter, "Health and Self-Care for Single Parents," illuminates the path towards a healthier and happier you. It's a gentle reminder that caring for yourself is not a luxury, but a necessity. When your life is fueled by self-care, you're not just a better parent, you're a better you.

# Recognizing Stress and Burnout

Taking a deep breath, you brace yourself for the day ahead. Your mental to-do list seems longer than the Great Wall of China, and you're already feeling the weight of it. Between your job, school runs, cooking meals, assisting with homework, and everything else in between, the day seems like a mountain to climb. Yet, you do it every day. And often, you do it with a smile on your face because you know your children are counting on you. But beneath that superhero cape, sometimes you feel like you're simply treading water, trying to keep your head above the rising tide of responsibilities. If that's the case, dear reader, know that you're not alone. Many single parents find themselves on the brink of stress and burnout, too engrossed in their daily routine to realize the toll it's taking on their well-being.

Understanding stress and burnout is the first and perhaps the most crucial step in protecting your health. Stress, in short bursts, can be a positive force. It can fuel you to meet deadlines, encourage you to push beyond your comfort zones, and even boost your performance. But when stress becomes a constant companion, it can lead to burnout—a state of chronic physical and emotional exhaustion that can seriously impact your health and happiness.

Recognizing the signs of burnout is crucial. You might feel tired all the time, even after a full night's sleep. Perhaps you find it harder to concentrate, or simple tasks seem to take longer to complete. Maybe you're more irritable, snapping at minor annoyances, or find yourself increasingly cynical or detached from your surroundings. Physically, you might suffer from frequent headaches, insomnia, or a weakened immune system. If these symptoms sound all too familiar, you could be experiencing burnout.

But how does one reach this state? Burnout doesn't happen overnight. It's the result of prolonged stress and insufficient recovery time. As a single parent, you're navigating a sea of responsibilities every day—both visible and invisible. The visible tasks, such as cooking, cleaning, or helping with homework, are easily recognizable. But the invisible ones—worrying about finances, feeling guilty about not doing enough, or dealing with the emotional impact of your situation—often go unnoticed. Yet, these invisible tasks can be just as draining. In our society, there's a tendency to glamorize busyness, to treat it as a badge of honor. We often equate productivity with self-worth, and anything less than constant activity is seen as laziness. But remember, we are human beings, not human doings. It's essential to acknowledge your feelings and give yourself permission to rest.

One effective way to recognize burnout is through self-check-ins. Schedule a few minutes each day to evaluate how you're feeling physically, emotionally, and mentally. Are you feeling fatigued? Do you feel emotionally drained? Are you having trouble focusing? Identifying these symptoms early on can help prevent a full-blown burnout.

One more thing to remember is that it's okay to ask for help. Seeking support is not a sign of weakness. If you feel like stress is taking a toll on your health, reaching out to a healthcare professional can make a world of difference. It might feel challenging, especially with everything else you're juggling. But just as you prioritize your children's health, your health should be a priority too.

Recognizing stress and burnout is an essential part of self-care. It's about respecting your limits and understanding that it's okay not to be okay sometimes. You're doing the best you can, and that's more than enough. Remember, taking care of yourself isn't a luxury. It's the bedrock upon which you build a happy and healthy family.

# Simple and Effective Self-Care Strategies

Self-care—it's a term you've undoubtedly heard countless times. Yet for many, it remains an elusive concept, a luxury we can't afford, or simply the last item on our to-do list that we rarely get around to. But let me assure you, as a single parent, self-care is not just a luxury—it's a necessity.

Imagine your life as a cup. Each day, various responsibilities and stressors take a sip from your cup. Eventually, your cup will run dry if you don't take time to refill it. And a parched cup has nothing to give. The process of self-care is essentially replenishing that cup, enabling you to continue giving to your children and managing your day-to-day life.

So, where does one start on this self-care journey? Start with the basics. Make sure you're eating healthy meals, staying hydrated, and getting regular exercise. It doesn't have to be elaborate—simple changes can lead to significant results. You might consider a quick salad loaded with vegetables for lunch, drinking an extra glass of water, or a short walk around the block. It might not seem like much, but these small steps add up and contribute to better physical health, which in turn improves mental health.

Getting enough sleep is another critical aspect of self-care. Many single parents find themselves staying up late or waking up early to finish chores, thereby compromising their sleep. However, good quality sleep is vital for physical health and emotional well-being. Establishing a regular sleep routine can be incredibly beneficial. Try to go to bed and wake up at the same time each day, even on weekends. This helps regulate your body's internal clock and can make it easier to fall asleep and wake up.

Another self-care strategy involves making time for activities you enjoy. Find what lights up your soul and brings you joy, then set aside some time each week for it. This could be anything from reading a book, gardening, painting, or simply sitting quietly with a cup of coffee. Even if it's just for fifteen minutes, this "me time" can be an oasis of calm in the midst of a hectic day.

Mindfulness can be a powerful tool for self-care. It involves being present in the moment, acknowledging and accepting your feelings without judgment. By incorporating mindfulness into your routine, you can become more aware of your stressors and better equipped to handle them. You don't need any special equipment or a lot of time to practice mindfulness — it can be as simple as focusing on your breath for a few minutes each day.

Then there is the practice of gratitude. Though it may seem counterintuitive, especially when you're overwhelmed, acknowledging what you're thankful for can shift your perspective and bring positivity into your life. It doesn't have to be grand; appreciating simple things, like a child's laughter or a sunny day, can bring immense joy.

Lastly, remember that it's okay to lean on others. Building a support network can provide emotional relief and practical help when you need it. This could be family, friends, or even a single parent support group. Asking for help is not a sign of weakness; it's a sign of strength. It shows that you recognize your limits and respect your well-being.

Self-care is not about grand gestures or expensive spa days. It's about taking small steps each day to care for your body, mind, and spirit. It's about acknowledging your worth and understanding that you cannot pour from an empty cup. It's about making yourself a priority, because when you take care of yourself, you're in a better position to take care of your children. Remember, you deserve care and compassion as much as anyone else in your life. And as a single parent, that care has to start with you.

# Fostering Mental Health and Wellbeing

In the journey of single parenthood, while physical health is vitally important, mental health holds equal, if not more, significance. Mental well-being is the framework that supports all aspects of life, from how we think and feel to how we act and react. Our mental health shapes our perspective, steers our relationships, and guides our decisions.

When you are thriving mentally, you have the capacity to be fully present and engaged in life. You can deal with life's adversities, work productively, make meaningful contributions to your community, and foster a positive environment for your child.

Mental health, however, is not just the absence of mental illness. It involves maintaining a balanced mental state, where feelings of happiness, contentment, and accomplishment outweigh stress, worry, and sadness. As a single parent, it's common to experience heightened stress and challenges that can strain your mental health. Hence, fostering mental wellbeing becomes crucial.

To begin nurturing your mental health, take time each day for reflection and self-awareness. Check-in with your feelings, identify any sources of stress, and assess your coping strategies. By understanding what's happening inside, you can take proactive steps to manage your mental health.

Cultivating a positive mindset is another powerful tool for mental wellness. Instead of focusing on the hardships of single parenting, try to focus on the strengths and resilience you've gained through the process. Adopt an attitude of growth, seeing challenges not as insurmountable problems but as opportunities to learn and grow.

Another step towards maintaining mental well-being involves setting boundaries. It's okay to say no when you're feeling overwhelmed. It's okay to take time out for yourself. It's okay to seek help when you need it. Remember, your needs are just as important as anyone else's.

Practicing mindfulness is a beneficial way to promote mental health. Mindfulness brings you into the present moment, helping you to distance yourself from worries about the future or regrets about the past. It enhances emotional awareness, reducing stress and enhancing your overall wellbeing.

Mental health also involves caring for your emotional needs. This can be done through activities that make you happy, like listening to music, spending time in nature, or engaging in hobbies. Laughter is a powerful antidote to stress, so don't forget to find humor in the daily trials of life.

At times, you may find that you're struggling more than usual or feeling persistently low. If this is the case, don't hesitate to seek professional help. Therapists, counselors, and mental health professionals can provide strategies and resources to help you navigate your feelings and manage your mental health effectively.

Cultivating strong relationships is another crucial aspect of mental health. Connecting with others can provide a sense of belonging, reduce feelings of isolation, and provide a support system. This can involve spending quality time with friends, joining support groups, or participating in community events.

In the end, fostering mental health is not a one-size-fits-all process. It's a journey unique to each individual, requiring patience, kindness, and consistency. By prioritizing your mental health, you're not just caring for yourself; you're also modeling healthy habits for your children, setting them up for their own journey towards mental wellbeing.

As we close the curtains on Chapter 8, embracing self-care and fostering mental health, we make way for the dawn of a new chapter. This chapter is where the heart finds comfort, the mind finds peace, and the spirit finds joy. We turn our gaze inward to the world that we create within our four walls, our haven, our home.

In Chapter 9, we will walk through the corridor of creating a happy home environment. Because ultimately, the home environment sets the stage for how your child perceives the world. It is the soil in which their roots grow and flourish. A happy home isn't about the physical attributes or the material possessions it holds. Instead, it is about the emotions and experiences it fosters - love, warmth, safety, encouragement, respect, and happiness.

How can we design this environment? How can we transform our homes into sanctuaries of happiness and peace, not just for our children but also for ourselves? Join me in Chapter 9 as we explore these important questions, illuminating the ways to build a home that nurtures the hearts and minds of everyone who enters.

# Chapter 9: Creating a Happy Home Environment

When Laura Ingalls Wilder beautifully penned, "Home is the nicest word there is," she captured the essence of what a home represents. It is not just a physical space where we rest our weary heads at night or merely a shelter from the outside elements. A home is a sanctuary, a refuge, a sacred space where memories are woven, laughter echoes, and love blossoms. It is a dynamic ecosystem that reflects our inner state and profoundly influences our well-being and that of our children. As parents, it becomes our responsibility to mold this space into one that resonates with warmth, peace, and joy.

Creating a happy home environment is akin to composing a symphony. Each note, each instrument, plays a critical role in creating harmony and rhythm. In our homes, these notes translate to organization, routine, positivity, and harmony. We'll begin this chapter by looking at how we can organize our homes for efficiency. A cluttered home often leads to a cluttered mind, while an organized space breeds clarity and calmness. Practical, smart, and child-friendly organization solutions can make a world of difference in how smoothly our days run.

Next, we'll focus on the power of routines. Establishing consistent daily routines brings structure to chaos and predictability to the unpredictable. The feeling of safety that predictability brings to a child's life cannot be underestimated. In this section, we'll discuss how we can construct routines that balance structure and flexibility — ones that cater to our children's needs and our own.

Finally, we'll explore how to foster positivity and harmony within our homes. These two elements are the heartbeats of a happy home environment. We will dive into the ways in which we can cultivate positive interactions, manage conflicts with grace, and instill values of empathy, respect, and compassion.

Throughout this chapter, we will engage in an important journey, threading the beads of organization, routine, positivity, and harmony together to create the necklace of a happy home environment. Together, we will uncover the ingredients that go into nurturing a home that isn't just a physical space, but an emotional haven for us and our children.

# Organizing for Efficiency

The beauty of an efficiently organized home is that it operates like a well-oiled machine. Items have their designated places, essential spaces are clutter-free, and things generally run smoothly. Not only does this bring a sense of order and calm to your surroundings, but it also streamlines your daily tasks, reducing stress and increasing productivity. More importantly, it sets an example for our children, teaching them valuable lessons about cleanliness, respect for shared spaces, and personal responsibility.

As parents, we need not chase perfection in organization. The goal isn't to cultivate a museum-like environment where every item is painstakingly curated. Instead, our focus should be on functional efficiency. This means creating an environment where you and your child can easily access what you need when you need it. To start, identify the 'activity zones' in your home. These are areas where specific tasks are carried out. For instance, a study or reading corner, a play area, a homework spot, and so on. Tailor these zones according to the task, keeping all the necessary items within easy reach.

Children, especially the younger ones, operate best when they have visual access to their belongings. Using open shelves and clear storage boxes can help them locate their stuff quickly. Labeling bins and boxes enhances this further, aiding in reading and recognition for older kids. This can be a fun and educational activity to do together, decorating and personalizing the labels.

Another integral part of home organization is decluttering. This isn't just about removing physical clutter; it's about eliminating the 'noise' that excess creates. A home choked with unnecessary items can feel overwhelming to a child. Periodic decluttering, involving your child in the process, teaches them about letting go, sharing, and the value of simplicity. Plus, it creates room for what truly matters.

Efficient organization also extends to time. This means creating and adhering to schedules for chores, study time, meals, and even leisure activities. A visible family calendar detailing daily tasks, responsibilities, and important dates can help. Digital tools and apps offer excellent resources for this, too, but a traditional calendar, placed centrally, can serve as a constant visual reminder.

However, while setting up schedules, ensure you factor in some 'down-time'. Life cannot be perfectly compartmentalized into neat time slots, and some of the best memories often happen in the unscheduled moments of spontaneity.

Organizing a home for efficiency is a continuous process, not a one-time task. As your child grows, their needs and activities change, and so should your organization strategies. Stay flexible and open to revising and refining your methods.

Remember, a well-organized home can bring serenity to your hectic life as a single parent. It provides structure, saves time, and can reduce the feeling of being constantly overwhelmed. However, don't pressure yourself to maintain an immaculate space always. It's perfectly fine to have a little 'controlled chaos' now and then because, at the end of the day, a home should feel lived in. As we navigate through this journey of efficient organization, the ultimate aim is to create a home that facilitates growth, connection, and the creation of cherished memories.

# Establishing Routines

When you hear the word 'routine,' it might evoke images of rigid, regimented schedules that allow no room for spontaneity or relaxation. However, when we talk about establishing routines in the context of parenting, we're talking about creating a framework that lends predictability and stability to both the parent's and the child's day. In essence, routines are about building a series of habits that guide our daily lives, leaving more room for joy, creativity, and meaningful interactions.

Routines are particularly beneficial for children. They provide a sense of safety, allowing children to predict what's coming next and thus reducing anxiety. This regular rhythm gives them a sense of control over their environment, building their confidence. Additionally, routines can foster life skills, as kids gradually learn to take responsibility for their activities.

To begin creating routines, consider the daily tasks that need to be accomplished in your home - morning rituals, meals, homework, playtime, chores, bedtime, and so on. It's helpful to write these down, roughly scheduling them into the rhythm of your day. While it's important to have a plan, flexibility is key. Overly stringent routines can create stress, the opposite of what we're trying to achieve.

Incorporate routines that encourage your child's independence. Even toddlers can help set the table or pick up their toys. Older children can be responsible for their laundry or preparing a simple meal. It's about setting age-appropriate expectations and providing guidance until they're comfortable doing these tasks on their own.

Morning and bedtime routines are pivotal. A calm morning can set the tone for the entire day, while a relaxing bedtime ritual can ensure a good night's sleep, which is critical for both the parent and the child. These times of the day also offer opportunities for bonding - a shared breakfast, a story at bedtime. Treasure these moments, as they build lasting memories and foster deep connections.

Integrating family traditions into your routines can further enhance their value. A weekly game night, family dinners, or a dedicated 'quiet time' for reading together can become beloved habits that your child looks forward to. They not only create a sense of belonging and continuity but also infuse fun into the everyday.

Remember, it's important to involve your child in the creation of these routines. This gives them a sense of ownership and increases their willingness to participate. Over time, they'll begin to understand the reasons behind certain routines, seeing them as part of a harmonious household operation, rather than arbitrary rules.

Consistency is the backbone of successful routines. It may take time for habits to form, and there will be days when things don't go according to plan. Patience is crucial during these times. Consistency doesn't mean never deviating from the routine; it means always returning to it, even after those inevitable disruptions.

Routines are not about creating a military-style boot camp. They're about fostering an environment where things flow more smoothly. They provide a comforting, predictable rhythm to our days, helping us manage our time effectively and reducing the cognitive load of constant decision-making. They create the structure within which spontaneity, creativity, and deep connections can flourish. Establishing effective routines is an investment in a happier, more harmonious household, and indeed, a happier, more secure child.

# Fostering Positivity and Harmony

In our quest to create a happy home environment, one element stands paramount - nurturing a sense of positivity and harmony within our household. This chapter seeks to guide single parents in fostering a climate that radiates positivity, inviting peaceful interactions and creating a nurturing atmosphere for the entire family.

Harmony in a household is not about the absence of conflict; it's about how conflict is handled. Children, like adults, have their own perspectives, needs, and emotions. Disagreements are natural, and they provide valuable opportunities for teaching children about negotiation, empathy, and respect for others' viewpoints.

A positive environment starts with you, the parent. As the principal figure in your child's life, your attitudes and behaviors have a significant influence on the overall mood of the home. Emphasizing the good, expressing gratitude, and maintaining a positive outlook, even when faced with challenges, sets the tone for a positive environment.

Modeling effective communication is another critical factor. Be transparent about your feelings without allowing them to overwhelm the conversation. Encourage your child to express their emotions and thoughts honestly and respectfully. Conversations should not be monologues but dialogues that foster mutual understanding and respect.

Establishing rules is important, but so is explaining the reasoning behind them. If children understand why certain behaviors are expected, they're more likely to adhere to the rules willingly. Setting boundaries while giving them room to explore and make their own decisions encourages independence and self-regulation.

A peaceful household is one where everyone feels heard and valued. Practice active listening when your child speaks to you - put away distractions and give them your full attention. Validating their feelings and showing empathy goes a long way in making them feel understood and respected.

Celebrate achievements, big and small, to foster a sense of accomplishment and to reinforce positive behavior. However, focus more on the effort and growth, rather than the result. A household where progress, persistence, and resilience are appreciated cultivates a growth mindset.

Another strategy is to make room for fun and relaxation. All work and no play can create tension and resentment. Fun family activities, laughter, and downtime can diffuse tension and bring everyone closer together. It's important to remember that a harmonious home is not just a place for responsibilities and learning; it should be a place of enjoyment and relaxation too.

Maintaining routines, as we've discussed, also contributes to a peaceful household. Predictability and structure can reduce stress and conflicts while giving everyone a sense of control and balance.

Finally, creating a positive, harmonious home environment is not a one-time task. It's a constant effort that requires patience, consistency, and an understanding that there will be difficult days. There will be times when rules are broken, tempers flare, and the atmosphere becomes tense. But as long as there's a foundation of respect, love, and good communication, it's always possible to return to a state of harmony.

In fostering positivity and harmony, you're doing much more than creating a happy home. You're teaching your child crucial life skills - emotional intelligence, resilience, empathy, and effective communication. These skills will serve them well in all areas of their lives, long after they've left the nest and ventured out into the world on their own. It's a gift that they - and you - will cherish for a lifetime.

The creation of a nurturing home environment, complete with efficient organization, well-established routines, and an air of positivity and harmony, forms the perfect setting for your child's personal growth and learning. However, the role of education in your child's development cannot be overemphasized. It is the conduit through which they gain knowledge, learn new skills, and cultivate a deeper understanding of the world around them.

As parents, we carry the responsibility to ensure that our children receive the best possible education. We guide them through their academic journey and provide the necessary support. Our homes and our attitudes shape the foundations of their learning, but formal education plays a crucial role in their overall development.

With this understanding, let's transition into our next significant topic: Education and Your Child. This chapter aims to provide useful insights into optimizing your child's educational journey, including understanding different learning styles, advocating for your child in the educational system, and strategies to assist with homework and school projects. Join me as we explore the many ways we can contribute positively to our child's educational experience.

# Chapter 10: Education and Your Child

One of the most critical roles we play as parents is guiding our children's education. From helping them with their homework to advocating for them in the school system, we are their champions on the path to learning. We have the privilege of igniting their curiosity, sparking their love for knowledge, and equipping them with tools for lifelong learning. It's a thrilling journey, and like all adventures, it comes with its unique challenges, particularly for single parents.

In this chapter, we'll explore the vast landscape of your child's educational journey. We'll delve into the inner workings of the school system, discuss practical strategies for managing homework and study routines, and discuss ways to nurture a genuine love for learning in your child.

Navigating the school system as a single parent can feel like a daunting task. You may wonder how to keep up with the array of school activities, parent-teacher meetings, and educational decisions that need to be made. But fear not! With the right resources and some handy tips, you'll find your way through this maze.

Homework and study routines are another vital aspect of your child's education. Establishing consistent routines not only aids in their academic success but also imparts essential skills such as time management and self-discipline. However, creating and maintaining these routines can be challenging, especially with the myriad other responsibilities you juggle as a single parent. We'll delve into some strategies that can make this process smoother and more effective.

Finally, we'll talk about how to encourage a love of learning in your child. In a world that often focuses on grades and test scores, it's easy to lose sight of the joy and wonder of learning. Fostering a love for learning in your child goes beyond their academic success; it lays the groundwork for a curious, open-minded, and enriching approach to life. And the beauty of it is, you don't need to be a seasoned educator to do this - you just need to be present, supportive, and open to discovery.

## Navigating the School System

It's a sunny morning, and you're standing in a bustling schoolyard, amid throngs of children in neatly pressed uniforms, clutching your child's hand. Their backpack, almost as big as them, is filled with fresh notebooks and pencils, and a hint of anticipation fills the air. It's their first day of school, and as you wave them off, you realize that this is not only a big day for your child but also for you. You're stepping into the role of your child's main advocate within the school system.

Navigating the school system as a single parent can feel a bit like finding your way through a dense forest. There are the straightforward paths like parent-teacher meetings and school newsletters, but there are also less visible, winding trails of school policies, extracurricular activities, and parent-teacher association (PTA) activities. It may seem overwhelming at first, but trust me, with the right approach, you'll be able to guide your child effectively through their educational journey.

The first stop on this journey is understanding the structure of the school system. It starts with knowing who does what at your child's school. Who is the principal, and what is their role? Who are the teachers, and what subjects do they teach? Who is the school counselor, and how can they support your child? If you're not sure about these roles, don't hesitate to ask the school. They should provide a directory or guide that explains who's who in the school and how to contact them.

Once you've familiarized yourself with the school's structure, attend school events and meetings as often as possible. These gatherings offer a wealth of information about what's happening in the school and how it affects your child. Parent-teacher meetings, in particular, provide crucial insights into your child's academic performance and behavior. Make the most of these meetings by preparing questions beforehand about any concerns you may have. Remember, you are your child's advocate, and these meetings are your chance to ensure they're getting the support they need.

In addition to parent-teacher meetings, joining the school's PTA can be a valuable resource. PTA meetings provide opportunities to connect with other parents, exchange tips and advice, and participate in decision-making processes that affect your child's education. As a single parent, you may feel too stretched to take on PTA responsibilities. But even if you can't commit to a formal role, attending meetings when possible, can still be beneficial.

Extracurricular activities are another essential part of the school landscape. They offer opportunities for your child to explore interests outside the classroom, develop social skills, and build self-esteem. However, managing these activities can be a juggling act for single parents, with time and financial considerations. Take the time to discuss with your child which activities they're most interested in and realistically evaluate what's manageable for your family.

Beyond these practical aspects, navigating the school system also involves advocating for your child when challenges arise. This could mean seeking additional support if your child is struggling academically, addressing bullying issues, or negotiating adjustments to your child's learning environment.

It's essential to communicate openly with the school about any concerns and to persist in finding solutions. Remember, it's not always about knowing all the answers; it's about asking the right questions and seeking help when needed.

Successfully navigating the school system as a single parent is no small feat. It requires time, energy, and patience. But keep in mind that every parent-teacher meeting you attend, every PTA event you participate in, and every school policy you understand is a step towards ensuring your child's academic success. And that's worth every effort.

Remember, you're not alone in this journey. There are countless resources available, from school counselors and online forums to parenting guides like this one, to help you guide your child through their education. Stay engaged, stay informed, and most importantly, stay positive. Your involvement in your child's education will make a world of difference to their school experience and their future success.

# Homework and Study Routines

It's a typical weekday evening at home. Dinner has been had, dishes cleared away, and the comforting aroma of your favorite coffee fills the air. But the calmness of the evening is punctuated by a constant undertone – the sound of pencil scratching on paper, the rustle of turning pages, and the occasional sigh of frustration. Your child is at the dining table, hunched over a pile of textbooks and notebooks. It's homework time, and you're there to guide them through it.

As a single parent, establishing a smooth homework and study routine can be an ongoing challenge. There's a balancing act between offering support and promoting independence, fostering discipline while ensuring the process is engaging enough to keep your child motivated. However, these routines, when established properly, can lay the groundwork for lifelong learning habits in your child.

Start by creating a dedicated homework space for your child. This doesn't necessarily mean an entire room – it could be as simple as a quiet corner of the living room or a well-lit desk in their bedroom. The goal is to create an environment that's conducive to concentration, free from distractions like television or loud noises, and equipped with all the supplies they'll need.

Having a specific, consistent time for homework can help your child develop a rhythm and understand that it's a non-negotiable part of their daily routine. This time will vary based on your child's age, energy levels, and other commitments. Some children may work best right after school, while others may need some downtime before they're ready to focus. Listen to your child's needs and be flexible in adjusting this schedule when necessary.

One of the most crucial aspects of a successful homework and study routine is your involvement. While it's important to encourage independence, younger children will often need your assistance in understanding instructions or breaking tasks into manageable chunks. For older children, your role may be more about providing oversight – making sure they're staying on track and stepping in when they're struggling.

Remember that homework isn't just about academic achievement; it's also an opportunity to develop skills like time management, problem-solving, and self-discipline. Encourage your child to take ownership of their homework, planning out their tasks and making decisions about when and how to tackle them. This will not only ease your workload but also foster their self-confidence and independence.

Homework can sometimes become a source of stress for both you and your child. If this happens, take a step back and assess the situation. Is the workload too much? Is the work too challenging? Are there other factors, like sleep or diet, affecting your child's ability to focus? If you can't find a solution, don't hesitate to discuss the issue with your child's teacher. They can provide insights, suggest strategies, or adjust the homework load if needed.

Lastly, it's essential to approach homework and study routines with a positive attitude. Celebrate your child's efforts and achievements, no matter how small. Incorporate breaks for relaxation and fun, to keep the process enjoyable. Use this time not just as a means to complete school tasks, but also as an opportunity to spend quality time with your child, to get to know their learning style, strengths, and areas for improvement.

Homework and study routines may seem mundane and repetitive. But in the grand scheme of things, they play a critical role in your child's educational journey. They set the foundation for a successful academic life and beyond, instilling skills and habits that your child will carry into adulthood. So, as you sit down for another evening of spelling tests and math problems, remember that you're doing more than just helping with homework. You're nurturing a lifelong learner.

## Encouraging a Love of Learning

Learning does not cease when the final school bell rings, nor is it confined within the walls of the classroom. Indeed, fostering a genuine love for learning in your child goes beyond their textbooks and homework. As a single parent, you carry the unique privilege of cultivating this passion, of igniting the spark that could lead your child to be an eager learner for life.

In my own journey as a single parent, I have realized that instilling a love of learning in a child is not a one-size-fits-all approach. Each child is different, and so are their interests, learning styles, and motivations. But through it all, there are a few principles that I have found to be universally effective.

The first step is to lead by example. Children are natural imitators, and they often draw inspiration from the adults in their life. If they see you taking an interest in gaining new knowledge, whether it's through reading, enrolling in a course, or just indulging in curiosity about the world around us, they are likely to emulate this behavior. Make learning a shared activity. Include your child in your learning process, discuss your discoveries, and share your enthusiasm.

Encourage curiosity and ask open-ended questions. If your child asks, "Why is the sky blue?", instead of providing a straightforward answer, engage them in a conversation. Discuss their theories, guide them to resources where they can find answers, or suggest experiments to test their hypotheses. By doing this, you're not only encouraging critical thinking but also showing them that learning can be an exciting journey of discovery.

Promote a growth mindset in your child. Learning often involves making mistakes and facing challenges. It's important to teach your child to see these as opportunities for growth rather than failures. Praise effort over outcomes, and help them understand that abilities and knowledge can be developed through dedication and hard work.

Engage your child's interests. Learning doesn't always have to come from school subjects. If your child is passionate about dinosaurs, for instance, use this interest as a springboard for learning. They can read books about paleontology, watch documentaries, visit museums, or even learn how to sketch their favorite dinosaur. This approach can make learning more enjoyable and meaningful for your child.

Incorporate experiential learning. From cooking together in the kitchen to a walk in the park, daily activities provide ample opportunities for learning. Use these moments to teach new concepts or skills. This hands-on, practical approach can help your child see the relevance of what they're learning, increasing their engagement and understanding.

Remember to give your child autonomy in their learning. Let them choose books, projects, or activities that interest them. This freedom can give them a sense of ownership over their learning, making it more intrinsically motivating. However, remember to provide guidance when needed, and ensure that their learning experiences are safe and appropriate for their age.

Cultivating a love of learning is a slow, steady process. It requires patience, consistency, and a whole lot of love. But the reward is well worth the effort. A child who loves learning is not just prepared for school but for life. They will be equipped to adapt in a rapidly changing world, to seek knowledge independently, to face challenges with resilience, and to find joy in the never-ending journey of growth and discovery.

In the end, remember that the goal is not to raise a child who can merely pass tests and achieve good grades, but a child who carries a lifelong curiosity, a thirst for knowledge, and a love for learning. As single parents, we have the power to kindle this spark. And what could be more rewarding than that?

In this journey of single parenting, we have explored the corridors of emotional stability, the pathways of school systems, and the world of learning beyond the classroom. Each of these aspects, though challenging, forms an integral part of your child's upbringing, shaping their growth into a well-rounded individual. As you imbue your child with the strength to face academic challenges and a thirst for knowledge, it's equally crucial to equip them with the skills to navigate the complex web of social interactions.

This brings us to the next vital phase of our journey - Chapter 11, "Navigating Social Challenges." Social interactions play a significant role in shaping a child's identity, self-esteem, and understanding of the world. They are as fundamental as education in a child's life. And like every other challenge we have encountered in this book, it is navigable, especially when armed with the right tools and insights.

In the upcoming chapter, we will be traversing the landscape of your child's social world. From understanding the nuances of friendship, handling peer pressure, to the importance of empathy and kindness, we'll explore ways to guide your child towards healthy social behaviors. Prepare to step into the shoes of your child, see the world through their eyes, and equip them to navigate their social experiences with grace and resilience. There's much to uncover, so let's venture forth into Chapter 11: Navigating Social Challenges.

# Chapter 11: Navigating Social Challenges

Just as the leaves fluttering on a tree tell us that the wind is blowing, the interactions our children have with their peers reveal much about their social environment. The importance of such interactions in our child's development cannot be understated. In fact, these peer interactions play a critical role in shaping their understanding of relationships, their views on fairness and empathy, and their ability to address conflicts and challenges. The words of Desmond Tutu resonate with the essence of this chapter: "Do your little bit of good where you are; it's those little bits of good put together that overwhelm the world."

In this chapter, we will explore the myriad ways parents can help their children navigate the exciting yet often complicated world of social interactions. We will discuss the strategies that can prepare your child for healthy peer interactions, fostering friendships that can bring joy, learning, and a sense of belonging.

No discussion on social challenges can be complete without addressing the painful issue of bullying. It is an unfortunate reality that many children experience. We'll offer guidance on how to recognize signs of bullying, how to talk about it with your child, and the steps you can take to address it, always with a focus on preserving your child's self-esteem and wellbeing.

In all, this chapter is about equipping your child with the tools and understanding they need to navigate social challenges effectively and positively. Let us proceed with a journey that, though sometimes steep, is well worth the climb.

## Preparing Your Child for Peer Interactions

As parents, we dream of our children flourishing in their social interactions, forging strong, joyful connections that will form the foundations of lifelong friendships. But as the world of playdates and playgrounds unfolds, it quickly becomes apparent that the journey towards successful peer interactions requires preparation and guidance.

Let's begin by understanding the significance of peer interactions. For our children, their friendships and daily interactions with their peers are not simply about fun and games. These engagements serve as their first steps into the world of social dynamics, a world that can be as complicated as it is rewarding. The lessons learned during these early interactions often set the tone for future relationships and social skills. As parents, we have a unique opportunity to help our children make the most of these interactions and to face the challenges that they may pose.

One of the crucial factors in preparing your child for peer interactions is the development of communication skills. Language is the vehicle through which our thoughts and feelings are expressed. When children can communicate effectively, they are better equipped to express their needs, understand others, and navigate the complexities of social situations. This begins at home, with you, their first conversation partner. Engage your child in dialogues, ask open-ended questions, encourage them to share their feelings, and teach them the power of active listening. A well-rounded communication skill set forms a solid foundation for successful peer interactions.

Social etiquette is another key aspect of preparation. This includes teaching your child about manners, respecting personal space, sharing, and other important aspects of social behavior. When children understand these norms, they can interact with their peers in a more harmonious manner. As parents, we must model these behaviors ourselves, showing our children that respecting others and maintaining decorum are not just rules but ways of life.

Another essential component in preparing your child for peer interactions is fostering emotional intelligence. Emotional intelligence entails understanding and managing our own emotions and empathizing with the emotions of others. By helping your child recognize and express their feelings, and by showing empathy towards their emotions, we teach them how to interact with others empathetically. It is also important to discuss different emotions and situations that they might encounter in their interactions with their peers. By doing this, we help them anticipate and prepare for a variety of social scenarios.

Confidence plays a significant role in successful peer interactions. When children believe in themselves, they are more likely to approach social situations positively and assertively. We can help build our children's confidence by acknowledging their efforts, encouraging their attempts at independence, and maintaining a supportive and loving environment at home.

In conclusion, preparing your child for peer interactions is about equipping them with the necessary skills and understanding to engage with their peers in a positive, respectful, and meaningful way. It's a process that requires time, patience, and conscious effort, but it's an endeavor that holds invaluable benefits for your child's social and emotional development. Remember, as you guide your child through this journey, your love, understanding, and encouragement can make all the difference.

# Addressing Bullying

Among the various challenges our children may face in their social journeys, bullying is one that, regrettably, needs our immediate attention. It's a harsh reality that has the potential to profoundly impact a child's emotional wellbeing and development. As parents, our role in addressing bullying is essential – not only in terms of helping our children navigate through such incidents, should they arise, but also in preventing them.

It starts with awareness, with educating ourselves and our children about the nature and impact of bullying. Bullying can manifest in several forms, physical and emotional, overt and covert. It can occur in school, during extracurricular activities, and increasingly, online. Each form of bullying carries its unique implications, but they all share the same underlying harm – they seek to undermine a child's sense of self and security. Knowledge is power, and when we understand what bullying looks like, we are better equipped to identify it, address it, and equip our children with the skills they need to handle it.

Addressing bullying also involves fostering a strong, open communication bond with our children. When our children feel comfortable sharing their day-to-day experiences with us, including their worries and fears, they are more likely to speak up about bullying. These conversations aren't always easy to start, and they might not be straightforward. As parents, we need to be patient, approachable, and attentive, demonstrating our readiness to listen and provide support.

As we guide our children on how to respond to bullying, it's important to underscore the value of courage over confrontation. Encourage them to speak up, to assertively express that the bullying behavior is unwelcome, but always within the confines of safety and respect. Equipping our children with self-affirming language helps them confront bullying while maintaining their dignity and self-respect.

On the other hand, we need to also teach our children about the power of seeking help. There is no shame in reaching out to trusted adults, be it parents, teachers, or school counselors, when faced with bullying. It's a mark of strength and assertiveness, an act that can often bring the necessary intervention to stop the bullying.

While addressing incidents of bullying, we must also consider the role of empathy and kindness in prevention. Teaching our children about the importance of respecting diversity, appreciating individual differences, and showing empathy towards others is crucial in cultivating a nurturing, inclusive environment where bullying finds no place.

Additionally, schools play a significant role in addressing bullying. Establishing strong communication with your child's school and understanding their policies on bullying is an important step. Advocate for your child if necessary, and work collaboratively with the school to ensure your child's safety and wellbeing.

Addressing bullying involves a multi-pronged approach of education, communication, empowerment, empathy, and collaboration. It's a sensitive topic that requires our persistent attention and proactive engagement. However, in doing so, we equip our children with the understanding and skills to navigate their social world with confidence, resilience, and respect for others. After all, we're not just raising children; we're raising the kind, compassionate, and courageous individuals who will shape our future.

# Promoting Empathy and Respect

A pivotal step in our quest to help children navigate the labyrinth of social interactions is to teach them the principles of empathy and respect. These traits are not inherent; they are learned and nurtured over time, honed through experience and guided reinforcement.

Empathy, the ability to understand and share the feelings of others, acts as the cornerstone of compassionate behavior. It is the tool that enables our children to connect with their peers on a deeper, more meaningful level. It fosters understanding, diffuses conflict, and promotes a sense of global citizenship. On the other hand, respect, which signifies a deep admiration for someone elicited by their abilities, qualities, or achievements, provides the foundation for positive, healthy relationships. It teaches our children to value differences, acknowledge boundaries, and appreciate the individuality of others. As parents, we must first model empathy and respect in our interactions - with our children, with our partners, with our friends, and with the strangers we meet in our daily lives. Our children look to us for behavioral cues; they learn more from what we do than what we say. Therefore, we must strive to show kindness, understanding, and regard for others in our actions.

We can also teach empathy and respect through open discussions about feelings, perspectives, and diversity. When we acknowledge our children's feelings, validate them, and help them to understand that it's okay to feel what they're feeling, we're teaching them empathy. Similarly, when we expose our children to different cultures, beliefs, and lifestyles, and talk about the importance of accepting and respecting these differences, we're teaching them respect.

Moreover, encouraging our children to express their feelings, thoughts, and ideas without fear of judgment promotes emotional literacy. When children understand their own feelings, they find it easier to recognize and empathize with the feelings of others. Likewise, teaching our children about personal boundaries and the importance of consent fosters a sense of respect for themselves and others.

Books, movies, and stories offer a wonderful medium to teach empathy and respect. They introduce children to diverse characters, experiences, and emotions, prompting discussions about different perspectives. Through these narratives, we can explore complex topics in a child-friendly manner, helping our children to understand and empathize with characters who may be very different from themselves.

It's also beneficial to involve our children in community service and volunteering opportunities. These experiences can help them to understand the challenges others face and appreciate the circumstances and privileges they have. It fosters gratitude, humility, and a desire to contribute positively to society.

As our journey continues, the principles of empathy and respect set the stage for the next important topic we'll be discussing. In an ever-changing world, there's one trait that will serve as a lifeline for our children - resilience. While empathy enables our children to understand and respect others, resilience empowers them to face their challenges, recover from setbacks, and grow stronger with every adversity.

We've been talking about understanding others, but how can we prepare our children to understand and deal with the ups and downs of life? It's time to turn our attention towards fostering this essential life skill. So, let's forge ahead into the next chapter, "Cultivating Resilience in Your Child," where we'll explore strategies to help your child become not just a survivor, but a thriver in the grand adventure of life.

# Chapter 12: Cultivating Resilience in Your Child

"You may have to fight a battle more than once to win it." - Margaret Thatcher

Resilience. It's a small word, but it carries profound meaning. Resilience isn't about never falling; it's about the courage to stand up again every time we stumble. It's about facing adversity, learning from it, and coming out stronger on the other side. As single parents, we embody resilience every day. We stumble, we fall, but we always get back up, dust ourselves off, and continue for our children.

Cultivating this resilience in our children is an invaluable gift we can give them. It equips them with the inner strength they'll need to navigate life's storms and fosters the grit they'll require to pursue their dreams. But how do we instill this quality in our children? How do we nurture it, foster it, and let it grow?

This chapter aims to guide you through that process. In it, we'll seek to comprehend the essence of resilience and its importance. We'll explore the strategies that can foster resilience, from promoting a growth mindset to teaching our children how to cope with setbacks. We'll focus on the importance of perseverance and determination, two key attributes that intertwine with resilience, and discuss ways to encourage them.

Cultivating resilience in our children is not just about helping them survive adversity but teaching them how to thrive despite it. It's about raising children who won't just weather the storm but will learn to dance in the rain. As single parents, we understand the power of resilience more than anyone else. Now, let's give our children the same powerful tool to face life's challenges head-on. Together, we can raise resilient children, equipping them with the courage to face life's battles, not just once, but as many times as it takes to win.

This journey may not be easy, but I can assure you, it will be rewarding. Let's embark on this path together, nurturing the seed of resilience and watching it grow in our children's hearts. This, dear single parents, is our next mission. Let's begin.

## Understanding the Concept of Resilience

Resilience – it's a word that often comes up when we talk about overcoming challenges and adversity. We all aspire to be resilient, and as single parents, we want to instill this valuable trait in our children. But what exactly is resilience?

At its core, resilience is about bouncing back. It's about having the ability to recover from setbacks, adapt well to change, and keep going in the face of adversity. Resilience doesn't mean that we don't experience difficulty or distress. On the contrary, the road to resilience is often paved with considerable emotional distress. Resilience involves behaviors, thoughts, and actions that anyone can learn and develop. The ability to learn resilience is one reason research has shown that resilience is ordinary, not extraordinary. It's not just a trait that people either have or do not have. It involves behaviors, thoughts, and actions that can be learned and developed in anyone.

One way to understand the concept of resilience is to visualize a seesaw. Balance is maintained as long as we have enough resilient behaviors to balance out the adverse effects of stressful experiences. For example, let's say a child has learned to make friends (a resilient behavior), but then moves to a new city and loses his or her friend group (a stressful experience). The child's resilience would hinge on his or her ability to make new friends in the new city and thereby regain balance.

Children learn resilience both from us and the world around them. As single parents, we play a critical role in modeling resilient behaviors, providing supportive environments, and offering them opportunities to build their resilience skills. Resilient children are curious, brave, independent, and able to adapt to change and cope with stress effectively. They have strong problem-solving abilities, are confident in their strengths, and believe that they can handle whatever comes their way. Understanding resilience is the first step to helping our children build this crucial trait. We need to understand that it's not about avoiding stress or adversity, but about equipping our children with the tools they need to handle those inevitable challenges effectively. It's about fostering in them a belief in their ability to cope, to adapt, and to overcome.

It's crucial to remember that resilience doesn't develop overnight. It's a lifelong journey. But every step we take towards fostering resilience in our children is a step towards equipping them for the realities of life. It's a step towards raising children who are not just survivors but thrivers. Let's keep this in mind as we move forward to explore strategies for building resilience in our children. Remember, we're not just raising children; we're raising future adults. And resilience is a vital tool they'll need in their adult lives.

# Strategies for Building Resilience in Children

As single parents, there is nothing more we desire than to see our children thrive in the face of life's challenges. After having grasped the concept of resilience, it's now time for us to explore practical strategies to build this trait in our children.

Foster Strong Relationships: One of the foundations of resilience is having supportive and caring relationships. Encourage your child to build strong connections with family members, friends, and other adults in their life. As a parent, provide an environment of love, trust, and consistent support. Let them know they are not alone and that they have a safe space in you.

Encourage Healthy Risk-Taking: It's natural to want to protect our children from the hardships of life but overprotecting them can hinder their ability to develop resilience. Allow your child to take appropriate risks, whether it's trying out for the school play or climbing a slightly challenging playground structure. These experiences teach them about success, failure, and the ability to try again.

Equip Them with Problem-Solving Skills: Resilient individuals are good problem solvers. Teach your child how to approach challenges logically and calmly. Encourage them to brainstorm solutions, weigh their options, and make decisions. This can start with simple issues like a puzzle or a disagreement with a friend, gradually moving to more complex situations.

Teach Emotional Regulation: Understanding and managing emotions is a crucial aspect of resilience. Provide tools for your child to express their feelings in a healthy way. This can include talking about their feelings, deep breathing exercises, or engaging in physical activities to manage stress.

Foster a Growth Mindset: A growth mindset – the belief that abilities and intelligence can be developed – is a key factor in resilience. Encourage your child to view challenges as opportunities to learn, not as insurmountable obstacles. Praise their efforts and progress, not just their achievements, to reinforce this mindset.

Help Them Find Their Purpose: Resilient individuals often have a clear sense of purpose that helps them navigate life's challenges. This purpose can be something big, like a career goal, or something small, like being a good friend. Help your child discover and pursue their passions and interests.

Develop Their Self-Esteem: A healthy self-esteem gives children the confidence to face challenges head-on. Celebrate their unique strengths and accomplishments and remind them of their worth regularly.

Model Resilience: Children learn by observing the adults in their lives. By demonstrating resilience in your own life, you serve as a powerful role model. Share your struggles and how you've overcome them and let them see how you manage stress and setbacks.

Encourage Physical Activity: Regular physical activity is not just good for physical health but for mental health as well. It can help reduce feelings of anxiety and improve mood, thereby contributing to resilience.

Cultivate Optimism: While we cannot shield our children from the hardships of life, we can teach them to maintain a hopeful outlook. Encourage them to look for the good even in difficult situations.

Building resilience is not a one-size-fits-all process. Each child is unique, with their strengths, weaknesses, and ways of dealing with stress. As such, the strategies that work best may vary from child to child. What matters most is our continuous effort, patience, and unwavering support for our children as we guide them in their journey towards resilience.

## Encouraging Perseverance and Determination

Perseverance and determination are the fuel for resilience. They are what allow a child to keep going, to continue striving and believing even when things are difficult. But how do we foster these powerful traits in our children?

Set Realistic Goals: Encourage your child to set achievable goals for themselves. These could range from improving a grade in a certain subject, learning a new skill, or building better friendships. With every small goal reached, they learn the value of perseverance and determination.

Celebrate Effort, Not Just Results: Rewarding effort instead of results teaches children that it's the journey, not the destination, that matters most. This can significantly boost their willingness to persist in the face of obstacles, knowing that their efforts are seen and valued.

Reinforce the Idea of 'Yet': The word 'yet' is powerful. When your child says they can't do something, remind them to add 'yet' to the end of their sentence. This fosters a mindset that sees difficulties not as definitive limitations, but as temporary hurdles.

Share Stories of Perseverance: Share stories of people who have demonstrated perseverance and determination in overcoming adversity. These could be stories from your own life, biographies, or fictional tales.

Encourage Healthy Competition: Healthy competition can drive a child to push their boundaries and persist even when they face setbacks. However, it's essential to emphasize that their worth is not determined by winning or losing but by their effort and resilience.

Teach Them to Cope with Failure: Failure is an inevitable part of life and knowing how to cope with it is essential for perseverance. Encourage your child to see failure as a learning opportunity. This can help them feel less discouraged when they encounter setbacks and more motivated to keep trying.

Help Them Manage Their Time: Good time management skills can make daunting tasks seem more manageable, thereby encouraging perseverance. Teach your child how to break tasks into manageable chunks, prioritize, and create a workable schedule.

Encourage Them to Seek Help When Needed: Let your child know that asking for help is not a sign of weakness but a strategy for overcoming obstacles. It's important they understand that everyone needs help sometimes and that it's okay to ask for it.

Practice Patience: Children learn patience by watching us. Show patience in your daily life and let them see that good things often require time.

Provide Stability: A stable environment provides a child with a safe platform from which they can take risks, persevere, and learn.

Perseverance and determination, like resilience, are not traits that develop overnight. They require consistent effort, patience, and support. Remember, as we guide our children, it's not about making them resistant to failure or adversity. Rather, it's about equipping them with the mindset and skills to bounce back when they face these inevitable life challenges. And in the process, we aren't just raising resilient children; we're nurturing future adults who have the courage to strive, the grit to persist, and the resilience to thrive. Having spent significant time delving into resilience, perseverance, and determination, it's evident that these traits form an essential part of a child's emotional toolkit. They are the foundation for a child's ability to adapt and thrive in the face of adversity.

As we turn the page, we step into a realm that challenges societal norms and opens up a world of new perspectives. We turn our attention to the men who play a crucial dual role, handling not just the challenges of fatherhood but also the responsibilities that traditionally fall to mothers. In Chapter 13, we venture into the world of single dads, who are defying stereotypes, reshaping norms, and demonstrating in no uncertain terms that parenting isn't determined by gender, but by love, commitment, and the willingness to put a child's needs first.

# Chapter 13: Single Dads: Breaking Stereotypes

"The quality of a father can be seen in the goals, dreams, and aspirations he sets not only for himself but for his family." - Reed Markham

Single fathers sometimes seem like an underrepresented group. However, they are an equally important part of the single parent community. It's crucial to acknowledge that single fathers face their own unique trials, often woven around societal expectations, and layered stereotypes about masculinity and fatherhood. Many people still hold the outdated belief that men aren't as nurturing as women or that children always fare better with their mothers. These stereotypes can be hurtful and limiting, obscuring the fact that men are equally capable of raising well-adjusted, happy children.

The aim of this chapter is to bring visibility to the experiences of single fathers, shed light on the stereotypes they often grapple with, and provide useful guidance to empower them in their parenting journey.

We'll also share practical tools for successful single fatherhood. Because whether you are a single mom or a single dad, at the end of the day, it's all about being a loving, nurturing, and present parent to your children. To all the single dads out there, this one's for you. May your journey be validated, your challenges recognized, and your love for your children shine through as we break down stereotypes together.

## The Unique Challenges for Single Dads

The road of single fatherhood is filled with unique challenges, some of which are influenced by societal norms and expectations. These obstacles can sometimes make this parenting journey seem like an uphill climb. But remember, understanding these challenges is the first step towards overcoming them.

Societal Stereotypes: As a single dad, one of the most significant challenges you may face is dealing with societal stereotypes. Often, societal norms dictate that men are supposed to be the 'providers' and women the 'caretakers'. These roles can cause society to question a man's ability to provide the nurturing and emotional support that children need. It is crucial to recognize that these stereotypes are outdated and do not define your capacity as a loving, caring father.

Navigating the Emotional Landscape: It is natural for children to have a range of emotions about the changes in their family structure. As a single dad, you might find it challenging to navigate these emotional waters, especially if your child is upset or sad about the absence of their mother. It's essential to be patient, listen to your child's feelings, and reassure them that it's okay to express their emotions.

Balancing Work and Childcare: Balancing work with childcare is a common challenge faced by all single parents. As a single father, this can be even more taxing, especially if societal expectations pressure you to excel in your professional life. To manage this, you might need to consider flexible work hours or remote working options.

Building a Support Network: Many support networks and resources are often more targeted towards single mothers. As a single father, you may find it challenging to connect with support networks that fully understand your experiences. Try to seek out communities, online forums, and local groups specifically designed for single fathers.

Legal Issues: In cases of divorce or separation, custody battles can be incredibly stressful. Unfortunately, there can be a societal bias towards mothers in these cases. If you're facing such a situation, it's crucial to seek legal advice to understand your rights as a father.

Dealing with Loneliness: Being a single parent can sometimes be lonely. As a single dad, you might feel isolated from your peers, especially if most of them are in two-parent families. It's important to stay socially connected and find other single fathers or single-parent families with whom you can share experiences.

Addressing the Absence of a Maternal Figure: If the mother of your child is not present in their lives, your child might express the need for a maternal figure. This can be a delicate situation to handle. It's key to reassure your child that they are loved and cared for, and consider incorporating positive female role models into their lives, such as relatives, family friends, or teachers.

Self-Doubt: The pressures and challenges of single fatherhood can sometimes lead to self-doubt. You might question your abilities as a father and caregiver. In these moments, remember to be kind to yourself and know that it's okay to ask for help.

Understanding these challenges is the first step toward finding ways to overcome them. As a single dad, your journey may be tough at times, but it's also filled with the opportunity to build an incredibly strong bond with your children. In the next sections, we'll talk about how you can break through these stereotypes and foster a deeper connection with your kids.

## Breaking Stereotypes and Nurturing Connections

Breaking through stereotypes and nurturing deeper connections with your children requires intentional effort, dedication, and a willingness to venture outside of conventional roles. As a single father, you are in a unique position to challenge societal expectations and shape a new narrative for what fatherhood can look like.

Rethinking Masculinity: Stereotypes about masculinity often suggest that men are less emotionally tuned in than women. But this notion could not be further from the truth. Emotions are not gender-specific - they are human-specific. As a father, you have every capability to connect emotionally with your children, to empathize with their feelings, and to support them in their emotional growth. Foster an environment where emotions are openly discussed and validated, showing your kids that it's okay for everyone, including their dad, to express feelings.

Flexibility in Role-Playing: Breaking stereotypes also requires flexibility in the roles you play. Be prepared to wear many hats - caregiver, disciplinarian, cook, tutor, and more. It's essential to adapt to the needs of your children and respond to their requirements in different situations. This flexible approach will not only help you break stereotypes but also teach your children about the fluidity of roles in the family.

Open Communication: Create an atmosphere of open communication. Encourage your children to voice their thoughts, concerns, and feelings, and be open to discussions on various topics. This open dialogue can help you better understand your children's needs and wants, fostering a deeper emotional connection.

Showing Vulnerability: One of the most profound ways to break stereotypes and deepen connections with your kids is to show vulnerability. Admit when you're unsure, apologize when you're wrong, and express when you're hurt. These actions demonstrate to your children that everyone, even dad, has moments of uncertainty, and it's perfectly okay.

Learning Together: Taking on the responsibility of single fatherhood means you'll likely be learning a lot along the way. Share this learning journey with your children. This collaborative approach can strengthen your relationship with them and make the journey more enjoyable and enriching for both parties.

Maintaining Consistency: Children crave stability and consistency. Establish routines and traditions that provide a sense of security and predictability for your children. This consistency can foster trust and deepen your bond.

Nurturing Self-Esteem: Encourage your children's self-esteem by praising their efforts, promoting their strengths, and providing constructive feedback. Your role as their primary influence is crucial in helping them build a positive self-image.

Quality Time: Prioritize spending quality time with your children. Whether it's through shared meals, outdoor activities, or simple bedtime stories, these shared moments can lead to meaningful conversations and memories, strengthening your bond.

Respecting Their Mother: Regardless of the circumstances, it's essential to maintain respect for your children's mother. How you speak about her and handle conversations surrounding her can significantly impact your children's feelings and attitudes.

## Tools for Successful Single Fatherhood

Success in single fatherhood is achievable with the right set of tools at your disposal. Below are some strategies that can guide you in fostering a loving, enriching, and nurturing environment for your children.

Building a Support Network: One of the first tools for successful single fatherhood is establishing a robust support network. This network can include family, friends, other single parents, or formal support groups. This network will provide you with a safe space to share experiences, seek advice, and get the necessary respite when needed.

Practicing Self-Care: Being a single dad means juggling numerous roles and responsibilities. Amid the hustle and bustle, don't forget to take care of yourself. Remember, you cannot pour from an empty cup. Make time for hobbies, exercise, socializing, and relaxation. A healthy, balanced father is better equipped to provide care and support for his children.

Effective Time Management: As a single father, you'll find that time is a precious commodity. Effective time management is crucial to balance work, parenting responsibilities, and personal time. Develop schedules and routines, delegate tasks where possible, and use tools like planners or apps to stay organized.

Financial Planning: Raising a child single-handedly can have significant financial implications. Budgeting, saving, and planning for the future become more critical than ever. Seek professional financial advice if needed and teach your children about financial responsibility from a young age.

Fostering Independence: Teach your children age-appropriate skills to foster independence. This training not only eases your burden but also prepares your kids for the world. They'll gain confidence, problem-solving skills, and a sense of responsibility.

Positive Discipline: Remember that discipline is about teaching, not punishment. Use positive discipline techniques that guide your child towards making better decisions in the future. Consistency is key in enforcing these techniques.

Open Lines of Communication: Maintain open and honest communication with your children. Make sure they feel safe and comfortable discussing their feelings, thoughts, and concerns with you. Regular check-ins and family meetings can be beneficial in ensuring everyone's voices are heard.

Education and Learning: Keep track of your children's academic progress and be actively involved in their learning journey. Help them with homework, encourage their curiosity, and provide them with resources for learning.

Respecting Their Mother: Regardless of your relationship status with their mother, it's crucial to respect her in conversations with your children. This respect sets a good example and ensures your children's feelings are respected.

Professional Guidance: Don't hesitate to seek professional help if needed, such as therapists, counselors, or parenting experts. They can provide valuable insights and strategies to manage specific challenges or situations.

Using these tools, you can navigate the journey of single fatherhood successfully. Remember, there's no one-size-fits-all approach in parenting. Be patient with yourself, learn from your mistakes, and keep striving for the best for your children. Above all, remember that the love and dedication you show your children are the most potent tools in your parenting toolkit.

As we move forward on this journey of single fatherhood, it is important to address another aspect that might cross paths with some families, a less welcomed yet a profound part of life – loss and grief. The challenges of fatherhood are not limited to daily routine, financial planning, or breaking stereotypes. Sometimes, life can take an unexpected turn, shaking the very foundation of our existence.

Loss - of a loved one, of a relationship, or of any significant aspect of life - brings with it a tide of grief that can be overwhelming. For a single father, the situation can seem even more daunting, as they are tasked with not only managing their own sorrow but also helping their child navigate through this emotional turbulence.

The journey of grief is a personal one and unique to every individual. However, certain tools and approaches can assist in coping with this difficult phase and facilitate healing. So, in our next chapter, we shall try to illuminate the path to understanding, managing, and eventually healing from loss and grief, all the while holding the hands of our little ones, guiding them through their own process of healing. Chapter 14: Dealing with Loss and Grief, aims to provide comfort, understanding, and strategies to those going through this incredibly challenging time.

# Chapter 14: Dealing with Loss and Grief

"No one ever told me that grief felt so like fear." - C.S. Lewis

Life, with all its vibrant colors and beautiful moments, also brings us face-to-face with loss and grief. From my own journey, I've learned that these experiences, while profoundly difficult, are universal human experiences. They force us to confront our deepest fears and challenge our resilience. This chapter isn't just an exploration of loss and grief, it is a guide to traversing these murky waters, both for yourself and your child.

Grief is an unwelcome but inevitable guest. It can arrive suddenly, on the doorstep of our lives, knocking us off balance. Or it can slowly creep up on us, shrouded in the guise of subtle changes that, over time, become too significant to ignore. As parents, our instinct is to shield our children from this intense emotional pain, to bear the weight of loss so they won't have to. But life is a journey, punctuated by joy and sorrow. Our responsibility is not to erase the sorrow, but to help our children navigate it, and in doing so, become stronger, more empathetic individuals.

We'll explore the stages of grief, not as a rigid roadmap, but as a fluid understanding of the emotional process that follows loss. We will then discuss strategies to support our children through their grief, ensuring they are heard, loved, and guided during this challenging time.

Finally, we will reflect on our own journey through loss and grief. As single parents, we often put our own feelings aside to focus on our children. Yet, to truly support them, we must also allow ourselves to grieve, to lean on our support networks, and to heal.

In the shadows of grief, it's easy to forget that we are not alone. Through sharing my personal experiences and professional insights, I hope this chapter brings a sense of camaraderie, comfort, and hope to those navigating these turbulent waters.

## Understanding the Grieving Process

When faced with loss, understanding the grieving process becomes of utmost importance. Grief, although unique to each individual, is typically characterized by a series of stages that we experience as we cope with the impact of the loss.

As a mother who has dealt with personal loss, I want to acknowledge right from the beginning that these stages are not a linear progression. They can occur in any order, some can last longer than others, and you might even find yourself returning to a stage you thought you had moved past.

We often refer to the stages as proposed by Elisabeth Kubler-Ross, a pioneer in the field of death and dying studies. She introduced a model known as the 'Five Stages of Grief'. They are Denial, Anger, Bargaining, Depression, and Acceptance. Although these stages provide a framework, remember that your grief journey is unique and may not follow these steps exactly.

Denial: The first reaction to loss is usually disbelief. Denial is a defense mechanism that buffers the immediate shock of the loss. You may feel numb, and everyday tasks may seem meaningless.

Anger: As reality sets in, feelings of anger often emerge. This anger could be directed at yourself, at others, at the world, or even at the person you lost.

Bargaining: During this stage, you might find yourself making deals with a higher power, promising to change aspects of your life in hopes of reversing the loss.

Depression: This stage is characterized by deep sadness and a sense of despair. The reality of the loss sinks in and you start to understand its implications.

Acceptance: The final stage is acceptance, where you come to terms with your loss. It doesn't mean you're okay with the loss, but rather, you've accepted it as a reality you need to live with.

While this model can help us comprehend the different emotions we may face during grief, it is also essential to acknowledge that not everyone experiences all these stages, and that's okay. It's vital to grant yourself the space to grieve in your own way, without feeling obligated to fit into a pre-defined pattern.

The grieving process for single fathers can become even more complicated. You are not only dealing with your personal grief but also need to support your child through their grief. It can feel overwhelming to juggle your emotions while also being the pillar of strength for your child.

It is normal to feel helpless and unsure during such times. It is normal to question whether you're doing enough, or if you're doing it right. Remember, there's no universally 'correct' way to grieve. Your grief is your own. Acknowledge it, express it, and most importantly, be patient with it.

When navigating this process, it's essential to be aware that healing takes time and it's okay if you don't have all the answers right now. In the upcoming sections, we will delve deeper into how you can support your child through their grief, and strategies to help you navigate your own. The journey of grief is a long and winding road, but remember, you don't have to walk it alone.

## Supporting Your Child's Grief

As a parent, our instinct is to protect our children from pain. However, loss is an inevitable part of life, and grief is a natural response to loss. As parents, our role isn't to shield our children from grief, but to help them navigate it. It is our responsibility to provide them with a safe space where they can process their feelings and heal.

When a child is grieving, they often do not have the language or emotional maturity to express their feelings fully. Consequently, their grief can manifest in various ways - changes in behavior, shifts in mood, or even physical symptoms. It's essential to recognize these signs and respond with compassion and understanding.

Here are some strategies to support your child's grief:

Listen and validate their feelings: Encourage your child to talk about their feelings. Even if they cannot articulate their emotions fully, your active listening and assurance that it's okay to feel the way they do can provide immense comfort.

Create a safe space for expression: Let your child know that it's okay to express whatever they're feeling. They may cry, they may become angry, or they may not display any overt emotions at all. Each child's grief is different. Let them know there is no right or wrong way to grieve.

Maintain routines: While your child's world has been disrupted by loss, maintaining a semblance of normalcy through routines can provide comfort and stability. Routine activities, whether it's going to school or participating in a favorite hobby, can give your child a much-needed break from their grief.

Provide simple and honest explanations: Depending on the child's age and maturity, you need to explain the concept of loss in simple and honest terms. Children have a literal understanding of the world, so it's essential to avoid euphemisms that might confuse them.

Encourage remembering and memorializing: Help your child remember the person they have lost. Sharing memories or creating a memorial can help the child feel connected to the person they have lost. It might be through photos, mementos, or even writing letters to the person they've lost.

Seek professional help when necessary: If you notice your child's grief affecting their day-to-day life or persisting for an extended period, it may be time to seek professional help. Therapists who specialize in grief can provide additional support and coping strategies.

I remember when I had to help my own children navigate their grief. I felt powerless, seeing them in pain, and often questioned if I was doing enough. But over time, I realized that the most critical role I played was to love them, listen to them, and remind them that their feelings mattered.

Remember, it is normal to feel unsure and overwhelmed when supporting your child through their grief. But trust in your capacity as a parent to provide love and support. This journey of navigating grief is not an easy one, but with patience, understanding, and love, it can be a profound process of healing and growth.

## Navigating Your Own Grief and Loss

Experiencing loss shakes us to our core and brings about an emotional upheaval that we, as adults, often struggle to comprehend. While we're busy taking care of our children's emotional needs, it's essential to remember that we too are grieving. My journey through grief taught me this critical lesson: we cannot pour from an empty cup. As parents, caring for our own emotional health is not just important for us, but it's also crucial for the children who look up to us.

When we lose someone, we also lose the future we imagined with them, the traditions we shared, and the love we received from them. We grapple with the impermanence of life, and our world turns upside down. The first step in navigating your own grief is acknowledging these feelings and allowing yourself to grieve. It's okay to feel sadness, anger, guilt, or any other emotion that arises. There's no prescribed way to grieve, and your process may look different from someone else's. And that's okay.

The following are strategies that can help you navigate your grief and loss:

Permit yourself to grieve: Many of us are conditioned to believe that we must be strong in the face of adversity. This often translates into suppressing our emotions. Allow yourself the time and space to feel your emotions fully.

Reach out to others: Connection with others can be a healing force. Sharing your feelings with trusted friends, family members, or a support group can lighten your emotional burden. Let them know when you need to talk, or even when you just need company.

Practice self-care: This cannot be stressed enough. Ensure you are eating well, getting enough sleep, and participating in physical activities. Consider activities that nurture your spirit too, such as meditation, reading, or spending time in nature.

Find healthy outlets for expression: Grief often brings a whirlpool of emotions. Find healthy ways to express these. You might want to write in a journal, create art, or engage in any activity that helps you channel your emotions.

Seek professional help if needed: Sometimes, the intensity of our grief can be overwhelming, and it may be helpful to seek professional help. Therapists can provide you with tools to cope with your grief and can offer an outside perspective when things get tough.

The day I lost my husband, and my son was the day my world changed forever. I remember feeling a deep void and a sense of disbelief that was hard to shake off. There were times when the grief felt unbearable, and there were moments when I felt guilty for feeling moments of happiness. Navigating my grief while raising children was challenging. But it also taught me the importance of being honest about my feelings, both with myself and my children. It showed me the strength of vulnerability.

The dance between love and loss, joy and grief, forms a part of our human experience. And as we navigate these seemingly contrasting emotions, we come to realize their intricate interconnection. In the journey of parenting, especially, we learn the profound wisdom embedded in these experiences. They teach us resilience, they bring us closer to our children, and they highlight the importance of cherishing every precious moment we share with our loved ones.

As we conclude our conversation about grief and loss, let's shift our attention to a concept that I hold very close to my heart - single parenthood. For me, and many like me, it represents the embodiment of strength, resilience, and relentless love.

In the forthcoming chapter, we will dive into the world of single parents, focusing on the unique challenges and unparalleled rewards that this journey entails. We will strive to explore and celebrate 'The Power of One: Redefining Single Parenthood'. This exploration will not only shine a light on the strength and determination of single parents but also serve as a guide to navigate this fulfilling yet challenging terrain. Let us journey together into this empowering reality.

# Chapter 15: The Power of One: Redefining Single Parenthood

"Being a single parent is not a life full of struggles, but a journey for the strong." - Meg Lowrey

As I pen down the opening lines of this chapter, I reflect on my journey, not just as a writer, but as a single parent. It has been a walk full of trials, tribulations, joys, and victories. The single parenting experience is a narrative that requires redefining. It isn't a sorrowful saga, but rather a testament to strength, resilience, and the incredible power of love.

There is an inexplicable beauty to the single parent journey, a kind of power - the power of one. This chapter is an attempt to highlight that strength, the unique kind of fortitude that single parents display every day. It's about replacing sympathy with respect, replacing pity with admiration, for single parents who are sailing in the same boat.

The journey of single parenthood, as I've experienced it, is a saga that unfolds in three acts. First, there's the act of owning your journey, accepting your circumstances with grace and courage. Then, there's the act of celebrating successes, big and small, that add sweetness to our struggles. Finally, we look towards the future with a heart full of hope and a spirit adorned with resilience.

This chapter is for those who have walked this path and those who are about to embark on this journey. We're not alone, and in sharing my experiences, I hope to empower you with the belief that, as a single parent, you are enough. As we step into this chapter, let's hold our heads high and acknowledge the power of one.

## Owning Your Journey

From my own experiences, I can vouch for the fact that single parenthood is an uncharted journey that's unique to each one of us. It's a path that demands a brave heart and an iron will, and the first step on this road is owning your journey.

We do not always choose our circumstances. For me, the transition to single parenthood was not an easy one. I found myself standing at life's crossroads, the terrain unfamiliar and the road ahead uncertain. However, it was then that I realized it was not about the path I had been placed on, but how I chose to navigate it. The initial shock and disbelief slowly gave way to acceptance and resolution.

Acceptance came in stages. First, I had to accept the reality of my new circumstances. Being a single parent was not a phase but a new way of life. It was about acknowledging my situation, understanding the challenges that lay ahead, and preparing myself to face them head-on.

However, acceptance is not about passive resignation, but an active understanding of your circumstances. It's about taking control, and not letting your situation control you. This is what I mean by "owning your journey." It's about standing firm and saying, "Yes, I am a single parent, and that's okay."

Resolution followed acceptance. Once I accepted my reality, I resolved to be the best parent I could be. For me, resolution was an action plan. It was a commitment to provide my child with love, support, and stability, regardless of the circumstances. The action plan involved financial planning, creating a support system, and learning to manage my time and resources effectively.

I learned to redefine my idea of family. A family was no longer bound by the conventional structures that society prescribed. As a single parent, my family consisted of my children and me, and that was enough. I realized that the strength of a family isn't measured by its size, but by the love and support it offers.

During this stage of the journey, self-care became vital. Single parenting is a role that requires you to be the caregiver, the provider, and the nurturer all at once. I had to learn to take care of my own needs, both emotional and physical, in order to be there for my child. I found strength in activities that I loved, and in doing so, I discovered new aspects of myself.

Owning your journey as a single parent is not just about accepting your reality, but also about embracing it with pride. For me, it was about being proud of my journey, and how far I had come. It's a unique road that each one of us treads, and it's time we recognized it for what it truly is - a testament to our resilience and determination.

Let me assure you, owning your journey isn't easy. But, as I've learned, it's the first and most crucial step in redefining your single parenthood. Because once you do, you realize that you're not just surviving the journey, you're mastering it.

## Celebrating Successes

As a single parent, I soon realized the importance of marking and celebrating successes, no matter how small. In the tumult of managing responsibilities, we often overlook our own progress, focusing only on the hurdles that remain. However, acknowledging and rejoicing in our achievements, personal or shared with our children, can serve as a powerful motivator on this challenging journey.

I recall a moment of self-realization that came early on in my single parenthood. I got my son ready for school - his school, get to work on time, and navigate my professional responsibilities with competence, all on my own. This was no small feat. It was a success, an accomplishment. So, I decided to celebrate it. I took myself out for dinner that night, relishing in the satisfaction of a day well-managed.

Celebrating successes isn't about grand gestures; it's about recognizing your own strength and resilience. For me, a successful day could be managing my finances well or having a productive conversation with my child about her school. On other days, success was as simple as managing to keep my cool during a particularly challenging toddler tantrum.

Celebrations, I found, could be simple too. It could be taking a moment to enjoy a cup of coffee, indulging in a hobby, or spending quality time with my child. It was about making time to relish these moments of achievement, to appreciate the journey, and to understand that each step, no matter how small, was bringing me closer to my goal of successful single parenthood.

With time, I learned to include my child in these celebrations too. As I marked my victories, I encouraged her to do the same. When she managed to master a difficult math problem or resolve a conflict with a friend, we would celebrate together. It could be as simple as a high-five or a small treat, but it was important. I encourage him to ~ foster him a sense of accomplishment, boosting his confidence and showing him the power of perseverance.

Moreover, celebrating successes taught us both to focus on positivity. In the face of challenges and setbacks, it is easy to forget the victories. But each celebration served as a reminder of our strength and our capacity to overcome obstacles.

What I came to understand was that celebrating successes was more than just a reward system. It was a form of self-validation and an acknowledgement of our personal growth. It fostered a sense of self-worth and instilled in us a belief in our abilities.

So, as you navigate your journey of single parenthood, I encourage you to acknowledge and celebrate your successes. Don't wait for a significant milestone. Celebrate every step forward, every achievement, no matter how small. This not only cultivates positivity but also serves as a reminder of your resilience and the progress you are making.

The journey of single parenthood is not an easy one. It is fraught with challenges and difficulties. But within these challenges lie numerous victories, countless successes waiting to be celebrated. So, take a moment to appreciate your journey, to acknowledge your strength, and most importantly, to celebrate your successes. Because every victory is a testament to your resilience, your strength, and your unwavering determination as a single parent.

## Looking Toward the Future: Hope and Resilience

As single parents, we are often so consumed by our immediate concerns that the future can seem like a far-off land, full of uncertainties. I've been there, and I want to share with you the lessons that I've learned along the way. Having hope and resilience is not about blind optimism; it's about faith in our capacity to withstand life's challenges and to construct a promising future for ourselves and our children.

There were times when I would lie awake at night, worrying about the next day, the next week, the next school term. How would I manage it all? The anxieties were numerous, but so too were my dreams. I wanted to provide a secure, loving environment for my children, and I wanted to realize my own potential too.

The turning point came when I realized that focusing on these worries was not helping me move forward. It was like trying to drive a car by constantly looking in the rearview mirror. I needed to look ahead, to plan for the future and have faith in my ability to handle whatever came my way.

The process began with setting goals, both for myself and my child. They gave us something to strive for, a beacon to guide us through our day-to-day challenges. These goals ranged from financial stability and educational achievement to emotional well-being and personal growth.

Next, I worked on developing resilience, the ability to adapt to adversity and keep going despite setbacks. This is not something that comes naturally to many of us, but it can be cultivated. I did it by focusing on self-care, nurturing my inner strength, and practicing patience and acceptance.

I learned to take care of my physical health, understanding that it is closely tied to emotional resilience. Regular exercise, a healthy diet, and adequate sleep became non-negotiable parts of my routine.

In addition, nurturing my mental and emotional health was vital. This meant seeking support when needed, whether from friends, family, or a professional counselor. It also involved making time for activities that brought me joy and relaxation. By taking care of myself, I was better able to take care of my child.

Patience and acceptance played a key role in my journey towards resilience. Not every day was a good day, and not every problem had an immediate solution. Learning to accept this reality, without losing hope, was crucial.

I also encouraged my child to adopt these principles. We worked together on setting her own goals, understanding that resilience is not just about bouncing back, but also about growing and learning from our experiences.

Lastly, I cultivated an attitude of gratitude. I made it a habit to acknowledge the good in our lives, the progress we've made, and the love and support we have for each other. This helped to foster a positive outlook, which, in turn, fueled our hope and resilience.

Looking towards the future with hope and resilience is a continual process, not a destination. It requires constant nurturing and adjustment as circumstances change. But with perseverance, patience, and positivity, it is a journey that can lead to a fulfilling and successful single parenthood.

As a single parent, you have the strength and the power to navigate this journey, to look beyond the immediate challenges and towards a brighter, promising future. Believe in your capacity to adapt, to grow, and to flourish. You have the ability to shape the future you want for you and your child, imbued with hope and fortified with resilience.

# Conclusion: The Journey Ahead

As we draw the curtains on this journey that we've shared in these pages, I want to thank you for walking with me. Thank you for allowing me to share my experiences, insights, and lessons with you. Thank you for opening your heart and mind to the possibilities that single parenthood brings, and for committing to making the most of this journey for you and your child.

The story of single parenthood is not a monolith, and the experiences shared here are but a single narrative in a world teeming with diverse stories. Your journey will be your own, shaped by unique circumstances, experiences, and dreams. Yet, I hope that you've found a bit of your own story mirrored in these pages, and that the strategies and insights presented have equipped you to navigate the winding path ahead with confidence and optimism.

In the pages of this book, we've explored a myriad of topics - from the immediate practicalities of budgeting and legal rights to the essential strategies for building resilience in our children. We have celebrated the triumphs and successes while acknowledging the challenges and setbacks. Above all, we've affirmed that single parenthood is not a detour or a dead-end, but a different path towards the same goal: raising happy, healthy, and resilient children.

The conclusion of this book does not mark the end of your journey, but merely a milestone on the road ahead. As you forge onward, I urge you to carry with you the spirit of hope, resilience, and empowerment that we've sought to cultivate in these pages. These qualities will serve as your compass, guiding you through the trials and triumphs that lie ahead.

Cherish the moments of joy and connection with your child, and treat the challenges as opportunities for growth. Remember that you are not alone in this journey, even when it might seem so. Seek support when you need it, and offer it when you can. Most importantly, believe in yourself and your capacity to provide your child with a nurturing and supportive environment, regardless of the obstacles that you may face.

As you continue to navigate your journey of single parenthood, I hope you will remember this book as a companion that shared your early steps, one that provided comfort during difficult times and celebrated your victories. The pages may end, but the lessons and experiences we've shared will, hopefully, stay with you, influencing your actions and decisions in your ongoing journey.

As a fellow traveler on this path, I stand with you in spirit, cheering you on, celebrating your victories, and empathizing with your struggles. There is no perfect roadmap for this journey, and there will be times when the path seems steep and treacherous. But, dear reader, never lose sight of your strength and resilience, your capacity to love, to endure, and to flourish in the face of adversity.

As we part ways in this book, remember this: being a single parent is indeed a journey for the strong, as our dear Meg Lowrey once said. And strength isn't always about not breaking; it's about standing back up, time and time again, braving the storms and basking in the sun with equal grace and courage.

The journey of single parenthood, like any worthwhile endeavor in life, is a blend of joy and struggle, triumph and defeat, clarity and confusion. Yet, every step, every stumble, every victory is worth it because, at the heart of it all, is the incomparable love we share with our children.

With this, I leave you with my best wishes for the journey ahead. May you find joy in every sunrise and hope in every sunset. And may you always have the courage to keep walking, even when the path is shrouded in uncertainty. The future is not a distant horizon but a story you write with each passing day, a story of love, resilience, and unyielding hope. Here's to the journey ahead!

# Epilogue

As we conclude our journey through Redefining Single Parenting: Overcoming Obstacles and Raising Resilient Kids, it's important to understand that your odyssey as a single parent doesn't stop at the last page. The challenges and rewards of single parenting continue to reshape and transform as you and your children grow and evolve together. This journey isn't about a specific endpoint, but rather an ongoing voyage, traversed one day at a time, empowered by grit, determination, and most significantly, love.

Following the path of becoming a single parent, I employed numerous strategies: family therapy, supportive communities, positive reinforcement, and time management, among others. These traditional methods provided a backbone of strength, but the most profound resilience emerged from a place I least expected.

In the midst of my single parenting journey, I discovered an innovative approach that bestowed a sense of calm and control amidst the chaos. This strategy, though not a panacea for all struggles, sparked a deeper comprehension of the parenting process and offered unique insights into fostering resilience in our children.

Enthused to share this newfound wisdom, I invite all single parents, or those on the brink of this journey, to explore this unique approach. Perhaps you, like me, will find it helps reduce some of the stresses, bolsters your confidence, and paints your parenting landscape with vibrant colors amidst the gray challenges.

While this strategy isn't a universal solution to single parenting challenges, it's a tool that could potentially provide fresh perspectives and coping mechanisms. It has been a beacon in my journey, and I am optimistic it can provide guidance and support to others on their path through single parenthood.

If you wish to delve deeper into this approach, please connect with me at dee.walterspublishing@gmail.com. Exchanging experiences and building connections with other parents have been instrumental in my resilience, and I hope it can be for you as well.

As you close this book and continue your journey, remember that single parenting is not a straight road, but a landscape filled with valleys and mountains. It's okay to struggle, to question, and to feel overwhelmed. But remember, your love for your children and your determination to provide them with the best life possible is your biggest strength.

In closing, I leave you with a promise and an invitation. The promise is that you are not alone. You are part of a strong community of single parents who understand your struggles and share your triumphs. The invitation is to reach out, share your experiences, and form connections. Together, we can navigate the complexities of single parenting towards a future filled with resilience, joy, and ultimately, a renewed sense of fulfillment.

Stand tall, for you are stronger than you believe. Carry your love for your children as a guiding light through the darkest nights. Know that every sunrise brings with it a new day, new challenges, but also new triumphs.

In resilience, determination, and love,

The Self-Help Hub